Bond Book ✓

This book is part of a special purchase plan
to upgrade the CALS collection. Funds for
the project were approved by Little Rock
voters on 12/11/07. Thanks, Little Rock!

Whose Gospel?

Whose Gospel?

A CONCISE GUIDE TO

PROGRESSIVE PROTESTANTISM

James A. Forbes Jr.

THE NEW PRESS

NEW YORK
LONDON

© 2010 by James A. Forbes Jr.
All rights reserved.
No part of this book may be reproduced, in any form, without written
permission from the publisher.

Requests for permission to reproduce selections from this book should be
mailed to: Permissions Department, The New Press, 38 Greene Street,
New York, NY 10013.

Published in the United States by The New Press, New York, 2010
Distributed by Perseus Distribution

ISBN 978-1-59558-397-0 (hc)
CIP data available

The New Press was established in 1990 as a not-for-profit alternative to
the large, commercial publishing houses currently dominating the book
publishing industry. The New Press operates in the public interest rather
than for private gain, and is committed to publishing, in innovative ways,
works of educational, cultural, and community value that are often deemed
insufficiently profitable.

www.thenewpress.com

Composition by dix!
This book was set in New Caledonia

Printed in the United States of America

2   4   6   8   10   9   7   5   3   1

Dedicated
to my wife
Bettye Franks Forbes
and my son
James Forbes III
who shared most lovingly
my pilgrimage of
faith and understanding.

Contents

Foreword by Bill Moyers   ix

Introduction   1

1. A Lifelong Course in Sexuality   21

2. Gender Equality: For God's Sake and Ours   47

3. Which Gospel Do You Believe About Race?   69

4. Economic Justice: Are All the Children In?   95

5. In War: Which Commandments Are Broken?   112

6. Critique, Confession, and Ecological
   Consciousness   131

Epilogue: Trusting God Enough to "Go Forth"   153

Acknowledgments   167

Notes   173

Foreword

Five days had passed. Five days since the planes appeared in the bright morning sky, the flames and smoke erupted, the skyscrapers began to tumble, and our hearts trembled at the realization that everything tied down was coming loose.

During those five days people who prayed to the same God and read the same scripture came to very different conclusions about how to respond to the terrorist attacks of 9 /11.

The founder of the Moral Majority, Jerry Falwell, said God had passed judgment on America: "I really believe that the pagans, and the abortionists, and the feminists, and the gays and the lesbians, the ACLU, People for the American Way—all of them who tried to secularize America—I point the finger in their face and say, 'You helped this happen.' "

His compatriot, Pat Robertson, the founder of the Christian Coalition, cried "Amen," denounced Islam as a violent religion, and warned President Bush not to be duped into thinking otherwise.

Their flame-throwing acolyte, Ann Coulter, called for a holy war on Muslims: "We should invade their countries, kill their leaders, and convert them to Christianity."

Across the country those sentiments echoed from one pulpit to another as conservative preachers sounded chords from the old hymn, "Onward, Christian Soldiers," as if readying for a twenty-first-century crusade against the whole of Islam.

But in New York City in the wake of the horror, as the debris from the attacks still smoldered and the survivors had only begun to grieve, an altogether different note was sounded at a remarkable event that offered an alternative to the wrath and vengeance.

In the historic Riverside Church overlooking the Hudson River, the Reverend James Forbes Jr. conducted an ecumenical service for people of all faiths, inviting them to unite in contemplation and meditation and to remember that "it is the absence of hatred that leads to peace."

The sanctuary overflowed with followers of Jesus, Mohammed, Buddha, and Confucius, along with Jews, Hindus, Sikhs, and others. But the theological distinctions melted as Forbes affirmed that each of the great faiths, in its own way, reflects the universal revelation of a transcendent God. He called on Americans to "join with one another and to pray with one another in order that we may discern a path to a more hopeful future than the misery and dread and suffering and death of the last few days."

PBS broadcast the service across the country to an audience as ecumenical as the congregation in the church. To his fellow Christians in particular, Forbes made a pointed appeal as different from the message of Falwell, Robertson, and Coulter as night is from day. "Jesus," he said, "revealed the capacity to affirm your own tradition and at the same time to reach out to those of other traditions," exhorting his followers, in his very first sermon, to move beyond "a nationalistic narrowness to discern the broadness of the heart of God."

The broadness of the heart of God.

This spiritual insight defines what James Forbes means by progressive Christianity, the subject of this book. It is faith with an inclusive embrace of the God whose embrace transcends and exceeds our own. Or as Forbes has been heard to say, God is like his mama, who doesn't think supper is over until the last child is seated and fed.

About so humane a faith there is nothing relativistic or fuzzy-headed. This faith sees the world as it is. After that ecumenical service, when a handful of detractors charged that the presence of Muslims was an offense to the victims of the terrorist attacks, I asked Forbes about the virulent strain of extremism that causes Islamic jihadists to want to do us harm. He answered: "There are members of the Islamic faith who are committed to achieving their ends by any means necessary and that includes violence, which I abhor. But there are Christians who are also bent on destroying certain other people—'Good old Americans' such as the Ku Klux Klan. As long as we can acknowledge that violence and terror are equal-opportunity visitors, and that they visit all traditions, at least we are not naïve in thinking that the only bad people are the bad people of another tradition." That's hard-headed truth-telling, not wishful thinking.

It was not the most popular message to be sounded after 9/11, but members of The Riverside Church have long been accustomed to hearing an unorthodox critique of prevailing mores from this pulpit. As Forbes's predecessor, the Reverend William Sloan Coffin had championed nuclear disarmament and once "solemnly and joyfully" declared Riverside a sanctuary church for refugees from Central America. Martin Luther King Jr. had preached from the same pulpit five times during the civil rights movement and, exactly one year before his assassination, returned to challenge once again the might and authority of the United States government: "If we do not stop our war against the people of Vietnam immediately the world will be left no other alternative than to see this as some hostile, clumsy, and deadly game we have decided to play."

James A. Forbes Jr. was a natural for New York's most integrated and ecumenical church, to whose pews came stragglers from every walk of life, refugees from the conformity of stifling dogmatism. "Your God is too small," Forbes would declare, "and so is our notion of what God expects." He dared to ask: "What is God thinking about in these times of war, when the gap between the haves and have-nots is widening and our rulers have abandoned the ideals of equality and justice? In such times God's heart aches and it is a sin to be silent."

But he never claimed to read God's palm, or speak God's mind. Once, as he debated the ethical implications of faith with the late Catholic theologian Father Richard Neuhaus, Forbes said: "I do the best I can to say, 'As I understand the nature of God's calling, this is an unjust act.' But while I strive to function out of a sense of Godly commitment, I would never presume to believe that God would say, 'Yes, that Jim, that's my boy.' "

He was, however, a preacher's kid born in 1935 in Burgaw, North Carolina. He grew up in the Providence Holy Church in Raleigh, North Carolina, where his father was the pastor. The family—there were eight children of whom James was the oldest son—lived in a three-bedroom home on Bloodworth Street. His mother Mabel was a domestic for a white family on the other side of the starkly segregated town. "From start to end," Forbes told me, "the predicate of race seemed to insinuate itself into almost everything until we thought of ourselves as a kind of spoiled batch of cookies. God made the other cookies, they were all right. But those of us who stayed in the oven so long that our pigmentation was dark, we were second-class citizens. We didn't believe it. But the power of the circumstances made it necessary to cope with that perception."

In spite of the obstacles, all eight Forbes children went on to college. James Jr. headed off to Howard University intent on becoming a doctor. Later in this book you will read of the extraordinary moment when Tchaikovsky and Eugene Ormandy "conspired," as Forbes would later remember it, to change his life. He completed his degree in chemistry, but then moved on to Union Theological Seminary in New York, where he taught for several years before being called as senior minister of The Riverside Church just across the street.

There his sermons mixed the vernacular and the scholarly. I was present one Sunday morning when, smack dab in the middle of a sermon, he broke into rap:

Wealthy getting richer
Poor getting poorer
Rats and homeless
Living in the sewer

Housing prices
Going sky high
Nothing to rent
And can't afford to buy

Spousal, parental
System abuse
Sometimes you wonder
What's the use?

Now I don't mean
To be uncouth
All I'm asking for
Is tell me the truth

What time is it, y'all
No time for foolishness

When he finished, the packed house—white, black, and brown—
stood and applauded. When he proclaimed "No time for foolishness," they knew he wasn't kidding. While challenging racism
Forbes also asked his congregation to think beyond race to the
realities of class, money, and power. "The truth is they are inter-
woven in the history of our nation. But the real issue that's facing
America is how do we justify a corporate officer, through his
options and his salary, making a thousand times more than the
lowest paid worker? If God were our consultant about economic
reality, I think God might say, in disbelief, 'You got to look at *that*
again.'"

He had to overcome his own heritage—the bias of the faith
and culture into which he was received—to take on discrimination against gay men and women. Riverside had moved earlier
than most churches to affirm an inclusive membership of straight
and gay. There had been some opposition. Now Forbes, with his
instinct for healing, tried to reach across the divide. "Many conservative Christians," I once asked him, "believe the Bible
teaches that homosexuality is a sin. You take the absolute opposite
position. Do you have anything in common with those people on
the other side of that theological divide?"

"Yes," he answered, "the first thing I have in common is that
when a person who is homophobic speaks to me I understand it

because I was, too. And the second thing is that I think they want to please God and I do, too. So we are moving together. For example, I tell the congregation about some parents I knew who had no place in their hearts for gay kids until they discovered one of their own children to be gay. The mother immediately announced, 'This is my child. Don't anybody go messing over my child.' The Creator had to know that among humanity there would be some gay people and some straight people and some people in-between, and the God who is revealed to me by Jesus seems to prefer that special attention be given to the child who is different, especially if that difference had occasioned rejection, humiliation, and ostracism."

I was there one Sunday in 2004 when Forbes preached a sermon that became so popular he was asked to repeat it from pulpits and platforms across the country. Its topic was "Politics, Plumb Lines, and Politicians." The metaphor was drawn from the Biblical plumb line, a "small metallic object, like a spinning top, with a narrow point to which you attach a string. Its weight allows the builder to see whether he is building a straight and sure line or whether the structure is deviating from the design. It's a measuring device, the symbol of a certain set of principles by which you can measure whether we are keeping faith with our base-line principles." Contending early on that the Bush-Cheney invasion of Iraq stretched the plumb line to the breaking point, he was criticized for meddling in affairs that are none of a preacher's business. He answered: "The church is perhaps the only institution in the nation that can ask, 'OK, how are our policies squaring up, not only with the principles of the Bible but with the principles found in the Constitution and the Bill of Rights?' Everybody else is scared to do it. The church had better be afraid not to do it. It is no act of unpatriotic negation to love your nation well enough to tell the truth about it."

In the pages to follow, James Forbes recounts a life that has never sounded retreat. To the contrary, his journey has steadily unfolded along that arc toward "the broadness of the heart of God." He has retired from The Riverside Church now, but through his speaking and writing—and that healing touch—he has found an even larger ministry, as ecumenical as always. His own life remains his best sermon, as we saw on that September day in 2001 when he called out the best from the great faiths that at that very moment seemed to be on a fatal collision course.

My friend and pastor of many years, whose visits and inter-cessions following my open heart surgery turned stumbling blocks into stepping stones, is all about new beginnings. To survey the wreckage of human affairs, whether on the scale of those ter-rorist attacks or in the tortured eyes of a suicidal member of the congregation who has come to your study reeling from loss, to look life squarely in its anguished face without letting yourself sink into despair, and to open your arms and embrace it, requires a faith throbbing with that sense of purpose exemplified in the ancient summons which came to Abraham: "Go forth."

And so the adventure begins that has no end, toward the broadness of God's heart. That is the meaning of this man's life, his message to us now, and, shades of Tchaikovsky and Ormandy, the great melody of this book.

—Bill Moyers

Introduction

In this book, I offer an invitation to you to join a spiritual awakening in our nation and to understand how Christians can partner with people of other faith traditions in addressing the many serious problems facing our country. I believe God has called each of us on a journey of faith, ever moving forward, guided and sustained by the Holy Spirit that leads us to healing, justice, and peace.

In the book of Genesis, we hear the call to "go forth," to leave behind the comfortable and familiar and undertake a difficult, unknown, and uncertain journey. God says to Abram (later renamed Abraham), "Go forth from your country and your kindred and your father's house to the land that I will show you. I will make of you a great nation, and I will bless you and make your name great, so that you will be a blessing" (Genesis 12:1–2). If we accept God's invitation to progress, to go forth on a faith journey, we become a blessing. Our cherished religious precepts and practices will achieve fresh blessedness as we journey in faith toward the not-yet-comprehended mysteries of truth and of love. But such a journey requires a willingness to leave behind some things we have known and to open ourselves to what God will reveal to us on the way.

As I consider my life, I look back in wonder at where God has brought me, even as I know there is so much more to be discovered ahead. Members of my own Protestant tradition, as well as other religious traditions, have accompanied me through various stages of my journey. My own journey has been to and through these various religious traditions, and through new and evolving faith-filled understandings of six key issues I discuss in this short primer on progressive Christianity: sexuality, gender equality, racial justice, economic class, war, and the environment. In the pages to follow, I offer my thoughts and insights on these topics and invite you, too, to be part of the national conversation underway about faith and values, beliefs and behaviors.

We are fellow pilgrims on the faith journey. We come from different places, and we are at different milestones on the journey. As we travel, we may find ourselves stopping for a time at an "inn," a place where, theologically, we rest and stay awhile. But these inns, like the various "isms" we may have subscribed to, are not likely to remain our final destination. We are summoned by God to continue to move forward on our journey of faith and discover new insights as we move through our lives.

Jesus was progressive. He was open to having his understanding of truth and love broadened. In Luke 2:52, we read, "And Jesus increased in wisdom and in years, and in divine and human favor." Much later, we find Jesus's own well-formulated religious viewpoint changed by a Syrophoenician woman who challenged Him after he first refused to help her daughter (Mark 7:24–30).

We all need healing and wholeness. We need to progress as individuals and as communities out of the brokenness, fragmentation, destruction, and disease in our lives and in our world. We are not on this journey alone. In addition to the companionship of various fellow pilgrims, rich and poor, black and white, and liberal and conservative, we are accompanied by the Holy Spirit. In John 16:12–13, Jesus reassures his followers, "I still have many things to say to you, but you cannot bear them now. When the Spirit of truth comes, he will guide you into all the truth; for he will not speak on his own, but will speak whatever he hears and he will declare to you the things that are to come."

When I consider the Spirit and the companions along the way of my life's pilgrimage, I am grateful for the many people who have helped to shape my present views. I know why I see things as I do and why I hold certain principles with such deep-seated conviction. You will meet some of these people in chapters of this book. They represent a few key examples of the many layers of dialogue that help us all move beyond childhood and adolescence toward the more mature future that we seek to reach.

AN UNWILLING MINISTER

I had no intention of becoming a minister. When I entered Howard University in 1953, I wanted to be a doctor. I was determined not to fulfill the prophecy of my family and my church: "He's going to be a preacher just like his father." I was intending to break the pattern of a long line of preachers in my family—my grandfather, grandmother, father, uncles, and an aunt—to pursue my love of medicine. Occasionally, when the disturbing thought that I might be destined to be a preacher plagued me, I bargained with God. I promised that if I were allowed to be a doctor, I would be a *religious* doctor like Albert Schweitzer, who became a medical missionary in Equatorial Africa. I majored in chemistry intending to apply for medical school. God, however, had other plans for me.

At the end of my junior year in college, my vocational direction took a sharp turn. That summer, before I could set off to an Air Force ROTC training program at Eglin Air Force Base in Florida, my destiny caught up with me. I was working as a part-time bellhop at the Francis Scott Key Hotel in Washington, DC, a few blocks from the White House. A guest who lived on the seventh floor routinely turned around and said to me as he left the elevator, "Young man, the Lord has a purpose for your life." Though part of me knew exactly what he was suggesting, another part of me insisted that he was discerning my vocation to be the religious doctor of my attempted bargain with God.

One evening that summer I attended a revival meeting in northeast Washington. The preacher was a friend of my family and, as a courtesy, I felt obliged to hear him. He preached from the King James Version of the call of the prophet Isaiah. The words that leapt out at me were "Woe is me, for I am undone" (Isaiah 1:5a). The preacher used a very homey illustration of what that phrase meant. He said he remembered one day when his children were eating molasses and they ran out of biscuits. They called to their mother for more biscuits. She told them they would have to wait because the biscuits were in the oven but they weren't done yet. The preacher seemed to address these words directly to me, "There are some folks like that: they are in the oven but they aren't done yet." At the end of the service, I told him I enjoyed his sermon. That was not the truth. I was disturbed; I had been exposed.

I went home, deeply challenged by the preacher's words. To calm down my nerves, I put Tchaikovsky's Symphony number 4 in F Minor on the record player. As I relaxed, the orchestral music was joined by a voice that shouted out to me, "Jim Forbes, don't you know I have called you? Yes, oh yes, I have called you." The voice made perfectly clear what I was called to do. I found myself repeating Isaiah the prophet, "Here I am; send me!" (Isaiah 6:8c). As I was yielding to the call, the music played on. I heard a conciliatory afterword designed, perhaps, to address my disappointment in not becoming a medical doctor. The additional word was this: "You will indeed be a healer, but it will be of a different sort."

I finally answered the call in 1956 when I consented to enter the ministry and decided to attend seminary. Following ROTC camp, I returned to Howard University and completed my degree in chemistry. For a year I taught science at Kittrell Junior College before entering seminary. One of the units I taught was Introduction to Botany. I remember my fascination with leaves, particularly the process of photosynthesis. I felt a special spiritual message in the way a leaf receives carbon dioxide and then releases oxygen.

The fascination with leaves would take on a much deeper meaning fifty years later as I settled into work after my retirement from The Riverside Church in New York City. I appreciated leaves as a scientist, but I came to think of leaves as having very special wisdom for members of the human family. Leaves open to the world in ways we cannot see. Their surfaces vary from smooth to rough and oily to dry, and they are amazingly diverse. However, they all combine chlorophyll, water, and elements from the earth. With the power of the sun and atmospheric carbon dioxide they produce oxygen. We cannot live without the precious gifts produced by the leaves. As I pondered the power and diversity of leaves, Ezekiel's vision (47:12) of a world being transformed came to me. Ezekiel had a vision of the tree of life with the leaves of the tree for medicine, for healing. The same vision as captured in Revelation 22 inspired the ministry I started after retirement. But I am getting ahead of the story.

In September of 1958, I left the South and made my journey north to study for ministry at Union Theological Seminary in New York City. My mother put two books in my suitcase: *Stride Toward Freedom*[1] by Martin Luther King Jr., and the King James Version of the Bible. She knew that Dr. King was a powerful role model for me. She hoped that his spirit would impart a prophetic dimension to my ministry where there would be concern for social witness as well as personal faith. I'm not sure why she gave me the King James Version of the Bible. Perhaps she hoped it would help me preserve my evangelical faith in the liberal atmosphere at Union Seminary, where they used the Revised Standard Version (RSV) of the Bible. One member of my family's Pentecostal congregation referred to the RSV as the Reversed Vision Bible. My mother knew that the Holy Spirit was a guiding presence in my life and that the scriptures I had learned by heart from the King James Version would sustain me on the journey toward a more mature faith.

My seminary training took me far from the traditional Pentecostal view of the Bible which is much more literal in interpretation and conservative in theology, but not as far from my family as might seem, at first glance, to be the case. Some of the preachers in our community specialized in condemning and excluding people who had sinned or otherwise offended the faith through divorce, adultery, abortion, smoking, or drinking. My father constantly urged people to aspire to live a holy life. However, I once heard him explain to somebody why he didn't rush to exclude those who didn't measure up to the highest standard: "No college I know kicks out all the students who don't make straight A's." My father had earned his Bachelor of Divinity degree from Shaw Divinity School in Raleigh, North Carolina, and had been taught the critical study of the Bible. He did not subscribe to rigid inerrancy theories. He did not really believe that a whale had literally swallowed Jonah. My father preached about the powerful symbols in biblical stories that could open our understanding and transform our lives. His was also a liberal spirit, focusing more on grace than judgment. His sermons were characterized by inclusiveness. Just as there was room at our family table for neighbors and strangers, he preached that God's table had room for all sorts and conditions of people. What I believe at this point in my life is largely a reflection of what my father taught me in my youth.

My mother's gift of Dr. King's first book, *Stride Toward Freedom*, proved to be truly inspired. I was deeply impacted by Dr. King's courage, wisdom, vision, and convictions. Even before I signed up for courses at Union, he had provided me theological and practical principles that became the bedrock of my theological development. Dr. King's emphasis on the social gospel stretched me beyond the personal model of salvation at the heart of the evangelical tradition in which I was raised. The emphasis there was on the conversion experience, personal holiness, and conscientious effort to bear witness to the saving work of Jesus Christ on the cross—His resurrection, ascension, and return. All of this would be derived from a literal interpretation of an inerrant bible, which would be the prime authority for faith and order. Within the Pentecostal tradition, there was an added dimension in the marks of faith. The experience of the Baptism of the Holy Spirit was a central element of formation in Christian discipleship. The gift of the Spirit was for empowerment for ministry and edification and guidance for the believer. In this setting there was usually vibrant and joyous praise in worship. I do not recall that in either the evangelical or Pentecostal churches there was much of an emphasis on societal issues or specific social concerns. Dr. King introduced a new perspective for me when he linked the social mandates of the Christian faith to the Holy Spirit. In his chapter on nonviolence, he spoke of the love necessary to be a faithful witness to the Beloved Community to which we were called. I remember the electrifying spiritual experience when, for the first time, I saw the coupling of the social gospel agenda with the work of the Holy Spirit (which had been the central theme of my Pentecostal upbringing). King said, "The Holy Spirit is the continuing community creating reality that moves through history." From that moment, I could not turn back to a personal spirituality that did not include the power of the Spirit in societal transformation.

The progressive spirituality I believe in is deeply rooted in the conviction of Dr. King that God's dream of the Beloved Community sets the agenda for the church. The Holy Spirit empowers and engages us in the work of building up lives and creating systems for peace, justice, compassion, and ecological responsibility. A faithful relationship with God cannot be separated from our relationships with the other members of the created order.

My original fascination with the power of leaves and my ministry to promote spiritual renewal would still not converge for several decades. However, an important milestone in my ministry occurred in 1984, when I spoke at a ministers' conference in the Church of the Covenant, St. Paul, Minnesota. It was a very cold day in January, and as I waited inside my motel room to be picked up, I prayed. On my knees, I shared with God how frantic and exhausting ministry was getting to be. I was doing a lot of coming and going, but I lacked focus. I asked God, "What am I supposed to be doing? What is the core of the ministry to which you have called me?" As I prayed, I gently clapped my hands to punctuate the urgency of my plea for clarity.

The answer came in a very strange way. In my heart I felt the Spirit saying to me, "I am answering your prayer in the cadence of your clapping." I was familiar with the experience of speaking in tongues, but I have never heard of the Spirit communicating through the cadence of clapping hands. I listened to the cadence and asked for an interpretation. This

time, there was no orchestral accompaniment. It was a rhyth-
mic reply: "The spiritual renewal of the nation is the task to
which I have called you." It was very clear that I would be a
part of God's team for spiritual renewal. It was not that I
heard a voice from outside myself. It was a deep impression
from within which took the form of a message addressed to
my soul. Such spiritual communication registers as con-
cretely and clearly to one's awareness as spoken words from a
friend. No strategic plan came with this clarification about
my vocation. Nevertheless, the reply pushed me to discover
what this calling entailed. I began to see that whatever I was
doing was a part of the unfolding of this assignment, even if I
did not feel or see its effect. I learned to trust that whenever
I needed greater clarity, it would come.

A DIFFERENT KIND OF HEALER

My post-retirement ministry has combined my work for spiritual renewal with an emphasis on healing. Not medical healing, to be sure, but a different kind of healing, a calling out to
people to become leaves of healing. In the Bible, botanical
metaphors often refer to people—"They shall be called oaks
of righteousness" (Isaiah 61:3); "His leaf also shall not
wither" (Psalm 13); "I am the vine, you are the branches"
(John 15:5). I could see the connection between the immune
system in the human body, which heals us, and our capacity
to have a healing impact on one another. I could see what it
means to be a leaf.

　　To be a leaf is to be conscientious about our own health
in body, mind, spirit, emotions, relationships, vocation, com-

munity, and environment. To be a leaf also means to make a commitment to being a channel of healing to others who need restoration, renewal, and healing grace. Congregations can become lush, full branches of healing leaves. As various modalities of healing provide their own special systems of care, our nation's comprehensive health care system will be strengthened by people of faith who are committed to being leaves that provide both preventive and transformative long-term palliative care.

The Spirit releases the healing power in each of us. The Spirit works within individuals and groups to build up the community of compassionate care. One of the signs of a genuine spiritual awakening is the increase of mutual care and the many who reach across boundaries to recognize our common humanity. As our nation faces much brokenness and hopelessness and as our economy accumulates trillions of dollars of debt, there is actually "good news." We have trillions of dollars of healing power in the human family. That power awaits release as we choose to lift the authentic gospel of divine love above the popular prosperity gospels of material wealth. Such materialistic gospels, if they can even be called "gospels," encourage the accumulation of material things without promoting the spiritual values of love, community, justice, and peace—a recipe for emptiness and debt.

Since childhood, I have been driven by the impulse to be a healer. I remember when someone fell down on the school ground and skinned a knee, I would rush over to try to offer a helping hand. Like a doctor on call, I felt it was my natural responsibility to care for persons in need. As I accepted the call and prepared for the ministry, I wondered where healing would fit in and what form it would take. I certainly didn't seem to have the dramatic gift of healing that I had observed in Pentecostal revival meetings. I was not likely to be an Oral Roberts–type healer or a Benny Hinn.

I was freed from speculation about what kind of healer I would be in the municipal auditorium in Jerusalem one Friday night in 1974. I had been invited to preach at a conference on the Holy Spirit. I was to speak on the last night of the meeting, and following my sermon, the world-renowned healer Katherine Kuhlman was to lead a healing service. The meeting fell behind schedule. I had to cut my sermon to an uncharacteristic fifteen minutes. I preached about a man in Mark 7:31–37 who was deaf and had a speech impediment. When the man was brought to Jesus to be healed, Jesus spoke the word *ephphatha*, which means "be opened," and the man's ears were opened and his tongue was released. I thought I did a good job, and the people expressed appreciation for the word I shared with them. After my sermon, Katherine Kuhlman came on stage and began a remarkable ministry of healing. All sorts of maladies were healed. As she was completing what seemed like a hundred miraculous cures, she turned to the preachers sitting on the platform and reminded us that we all could be healers. We appreciated her confidence in us but doubted our capacity to rise to her level of achievement. I must confess that I felt a bit jealous. All I could do was preach, but here was a woman with extraordinary spiritual gifts.

What happened at the end of the service has had a profound impact on my ministry ever since. A couple approached me on the stage and reported what had happened during my sermon. The husband had come expecting to have Kuhlman pray for the restoration of hearing in one of his ears. His wife explained, however, that while I was preaching and came to the word *ephphatha*—"Be opened," his hearing was restored in that ear. They said the Spirit led them to come and tell me what had happened. Later that night, I met Kuhlman in the Intercontinental Hotel. She expressed appreciation for my sermon and then she prayed for me, placing her hand on my forehead. I felt the electrical charge people speak of as being "slain in the Spirit," as when a healer touches them and they joyfully collapse into a state of spiritual surrender.

Later that night in my room, the spirit spoke to me that I was never to be jealous of anyone's gift. "If I want to heal through you while you are preaching, that is what I will do." Since that night, whenever I preach, I expect that perhaps someone will be healed in body, mind, or spirit. From time to time people will report on a very special healing during preaching or from the laying on of hands or from counseling or even from a word of encouragement while passing someone on the street. As I have healed, I, too, have been healed both through my preaching and in hearing sermons of others.

What I have been speaking of are personal religious experiences. There is also, however, class action healing. Dr. King spoke of the work of the Spirit as continuing to create and build up community. Spiritual awakenings can be felt in the heart, but a truly great spiritual awakening removes barriers between people and releases the energy needed to bring about changes in the whole of the society. In the following chapters on sex, gender, race, class, war, and ecology, I will be writing about that larger work of the Spirit.

Progressive spirituality understands that the Spirit that works in the hearts and minds of people is the same Spirit that widens the circle of inclusion in the human community and the whole of creation. The Spirit that heals our bodies also brings wholeness to the body politic. As a person of color, I have spent much time working toward racial equality. But the Spirit that liberates me does not get stuck on my issues alone.

One-issue liberation falls short of the Spirit's intention. Liberation extends to all who are bound. When we are set free from the prejudice of others, we must in turn be prepared to join in liberating and healing others or we will set limits on the full development of our own freedom.

Because my early healing ministry was focused on promoting racial reconciliation and justice, it would be unconscientionable for me to ignore other forms of injustice based on prejudice and exclusionary laws or social practices. I worked for racial justice because I had personally experienced the sting of racism, and I knew at the core of my being that God's table welcomed everyone without respect to the differences among us. Following that core understanding of racial equality required me to see also how women endured insults and discrimination. I also understood how deeply poverty harms our whole society. When I accepted the call to The Riverside Church in New York City in 1989, I stepped into a pulpit known for its commitment to peace, a commitment deep in my own soul, which had long been inspired by the work of Martin Luther King Jr., Henry Emerson Fosdick, Howard Thurman, and William Sloane Coffin. I accepted the call to this powerful, activist church to help it become more deeply grounded in faith and the power of the Spirit to make a difference in the world.

Soon I discovered that there was more for me to learn about the Spirit's profound love. When a lesbian couple at Riverside asked me to conduct a holy union ceremony, I wanted to say "no." How would I explain such an act to my family in North Carolina or to my ministerial colleagues in evangelical circles? I wondered what the professional consequences would be of my saying "yes." I performed the ceremony, but I was a bit uncomfortable. Earlier, the Lesbian Caucus at Union Theological Seminary had asked me to celebrate the Eucharist with one of the lesbian students as a political as well as a liturgical event. I tried to theologize myself out of these requests. I was not ready at that time to be identified as a strong advocate of their movement. With my own gut response running counter to my understanding of being a reconciling healer, I had to face my own bigotry.

When something makes us this uncomfortable, we probably ought to think more carefully about it. God works with our resistance, and it is OK to realize we have been wrong. We all have shortcomings. I was found wanting. I was forgiven. I am being transformed. If God only uses the few good people who are never wrong or never struggle, not much can get done. My friend Ardith Hayes has a T-shirt that says, "I may not be perfect, but parts of me are excellent." God does not will everything, but I believe God wills something out of everything, even the parts that are not perfect. So I looked long and hard at the contradiction between my response to questions of sexual orientation and what I believed about the love of God and the Beloved Community.

In Chapter 3, I will describe an event which took place in the early days of the church's development. Simon Peter, later named St. Peter, was led to a broadening sense of inclusion in the new Christian community; however, he had to go through a process of personal transformation before he could be trusted to join with the Spirit into new places of service. It was a strange and puzzling thing that made him consent to the new assignment.

Sometimes we are like St. Peter. We need a "thing" from heaven that wakes us up, reveals our resistance, and exposes how we shrink back from life-giving truths. To understand what God's word requires, we have to move beyond simple arithmetic. We have to do calculus. We have to be willing to take a quantum leap. Sometimes the Spirit cannot move us unless we are puzzled—not fully comprehending the tension within. I realize my homophobia was making me reject the security that God gives us—unconditional love. I was trying to establish my own security based on maintaining familiar boundaries against what I did not understand and what I feared. My own "no" caused me to resist God. Continuing to say "no" to God should be experienced as at least problematical. We say no to God at our peril, however. Working it out was tough, but I kept going back to God's table that excludes no one.

The gay and lesbian movement for human rights and justice was the "thing" God used to show me my resistance to offering God's grace to those who were different. It was a truth I came to understand when, in their presence and their reaching out to me in respect and love, I had to admit my limitations. Their challenge renewed my faith in a God who loves all of us and wants us all to thrive. As varied as are the celestial bodies and plant and animal worlds, so too are the members of the human community. Vast variety, united by common bonds, seems to be a cosmic principle of creation. How can humans be exempt? How can God not love all that God has created?

THE WORLD'S REAL ASSETS

Like the many diverse leaves that give us oxygen to breathe, I believe people are the real assets of the world, not money or possessions. We are the leaves on the oaks of righteousness, the leaves from the tree of life for the healing of the nations. Each of us can be a leaf, but to be a healthy leaf we have to take care of ourselves, not just physically, but also spiritually, emotionally, and environmentally. We cannot wisely care for ourselves if we cannot care for the earth that sustains us, and we cannot really care for ourselves without caring for each other. Even if we believe God loves everyone, we cannot assume that the bile and bigotry that still pollute our world no longer seep into us in some form—as depression or fear or pain or addiction or a stress-related illness.

When I was asked to deliver a speech at the Democratic National Convention in 2004, I worked with members at The Riverside Church to create a list of progressive prophetic justice principles for America. Using the image of a plumb line, a weight suspended from a string to hold up against the wall to assure that it is straight, I raised some questions about how we could evaluate our country's faithfulness to the moral and spiritual values of a truly democratic society. The principles I shared that night in Boston are key elements of a progressive vision that should inform our domestic and foreign policies.

According to this vision, when we are America at our best, we will pursue policies that reflect a strong commitment to the common good. No elite group should be so powerful that it can subvert the well-being of the larger community. The leaders of our nation will not rely on spin masters to deceive the American people, but will speak the truth. They will not give one reason for their actions when what they actually intend is some hidden agenda unworthy of our ideals. They will not lead us on a wild-goose chase pursuing objectives they know are not achievable. Policies will be intended to unite the country, as much as possible, to reduce polarization and fragmentation. Legislation will find a way to be good news for the poor, the elderly, children, and disadvantaged citizens. The Golden Rule will guide lawmakers as much as possible, reflecting their capacity to be empathetic to their constituents and the general public. The nation will distribute its resources so as to reduce the gap between the rich and the poor. A free press and the right of dissent will be safeguarded, and we will ensure fair participation for all in the democratic process. Our highest aspiration will not be domination of others but the achievement of a global vision of peace and productivity—restraining any impulse to imperialism. Finally, we must be aware of our responsibility to honor, respect, and protect our land, water, and atmosphere from pollution and contamination.

The outcome of the 2004 election did not leave me optimistic about our nation or about the healing of the nation. The principles I shared that night in Boston remain key elements of a progressive vision for our domestic and foreign policies. While many of us worked long and hard in subsequent years to hold our national policies to this standard, we have had to do so in the face of a government that favored the rich, ignored climate change, used our military for preemptive wars, and justified torture.

Since I retired from Riverside in 2007, I've had time to be puzzled about what will create a just society and peaceful world. I have had time to think about my call to be a healer that came in 1974 and 1984 and about those leaves I studied as a science teacher. That is why I have committed the rest of my life, however long it may be, to creating a society of leaves for the healing of the nations.[2]

With the election of President Barack Obama, we have awakened from a long nightmare. Though we face challenges more staggering than the Great Depression, which did not have to address climate change, terrorism, and a collapse of the global economic system, life is also more beautiful in its hopefulness. God seems to have lifted the veil of race, class, and gender to make us better able to see each other as human beings. Now that we have awakened, this is no time for foolishness or a slow start on this new day.

We face many crises and problems, but it helps to remember we can fail and pick ourselves up. We can sin and be forgiven. We can face real tragedy, real crucifixions, but our story is not the story of death as the last word. Our story is of resurrection, the power of life in us granted by the Holy Spirit. If we have a national resurrection, the dry bones of our past will be renewed by the breath of the Spirit and we can chart a new course for our children and our children's children.

This guide to progressive Protestantism reflects on six crucial issues for our day and what the renewing power of the Holy Spirit can do to heal our many infirmities and divisions. While it speaks of my own faith and the faith I share with many Protestants, I know from many years of interfaith work that other faith traditions also share the longing for the renewal of life and society. All our traditions call us to a vocation of healing and restoration.

The Spirit which knows no sectarian boundaries inspires us to make a brand new community, the Beloved Community, with room enough for all. The Spirit will not fix everything, and it will take some of us longer to accept the new vision. Nonetheless, the Holy Spirit will tether us to life and will tow or tug us toward the Beloved Community, and make us leaves for the healing of the nations.

A Lifelong Course in Sexuality

For several decades religious leaders of various faiths have sought to discern God's will regarding the appropriate expression of human sexuality. People in the pew have also struggled with this question, and even when governing bodies have advocated certain approaches to sexuality, individual congregations have sometimes been slow to comply with their directives. Ongoing discussions reveal deep divisions and strong resistance to new insights. Even after hard-fought battles that led to compromises among competing views, many tensions remain and the controversies raise pastoral problems for individuals and families of the church. Discussants on all sides of the sexuality debates may feel that their personal convictions have been undermined. Despite the stress occasioned by such conversations, these serious questions still demand attention.

A wide range of sexual practices and church stances calls us to remain in dialogue across our differences. Some congregations still deny membership to openly gay, lesbian, bi-sexual, and trans-gender (GLBT) Christians. Other churches welcome the GLBT community in their fellowship, and they enjoy all the rights and privileges of membership, including holding office, being ordained, and getting married. Will the same-sex marriages some churches perform be honored by other churches which do not allow them? What will be the response to the children of such unions, will they be welcomed in church school and youth groups?

Regarding both straight and gay adults, some churches openly accept premarital sexual relationships and post-marital sexual activity among the divorced and widowed. Some time ago, they also stopped considering masturbation to be a sin. On the other hand, most churches still experience conflict between their doctrine and their general acceptance of extramarital sex and masturbation. Some churches teach sex education as a part of religious instruction in the congregation and others avoid it or teach abstinence only.

Faith communities respond in a variety of ways to people who fail to live up to the church's teaching. Some shame and ostracize unwed mothers and fathers while others support them. Many ministers marry couples they know have lived together before marriage. Some pretend not to pay attention while others accept it as just the way things are. Divorce, infidelity, and even the use of birth control have no uniform Christian response.

Whatever position churches take regarding these issues, there is usually an appeal to the Bible to support the stand they take. Unfortunately, the Bible offers many texts about sex which can be used for widely differing understandings. A literal reading of the Bible provides patterns or marital arrangements, accepted then but not now. For example, some verses would seem to accept polygamy, concubinage, and levirate marriage.[1]

Policies about sex have repeatedly stirred up furors in the church. There are those who urge silence because they believe conflict and confusion about these matters weaken the witness and pastoral effectiveness of the faith community. Nevertheless, we need to pray, study, talk, and listen our way toward our best wisdom on these matters, or else we will be confused when we seek to teach our children about such matters. People of faith still want to know, "Is there any word from the Lord about my sexuality and about how faith can inform it?" Mature religious leaders will seek to respond with the most responsible perspective their faith has to offer. Avoiding the issue is not an acceptable response.

Here, I offer some insights that have been helpful to me as I've continued to wrestle with what it means to be a faithful steward of the wonderful gift of sexuality. I have reflected on many dimensions of my sexual life, first as a young child, then as a student, as a husband, as a parent, as a pastor, and as a teacher; the issues are always there. I would suggest that each of us is undertaking—whether we recognize it or not, like it or not—a lifelong course in sex education intended to guide us into the fullest, most loving, and most faithful expression of our sexuality.

I: THE COURSE

Welcome to the lifelong course in sex education. You may not have realized you were enrolled in it, but in fact each of us is a member of this learning experience as we discover what it means to be human, embodied, and in relationships with ourselves, others, and our God. From the pleasurable feelings derived from the caring touch of our parents, to the awakening of powerful adolescent urges and the longings of physical and emotional attraction, through the adult bonds of self-giving in body, mind, and spirit—we are all in the class.

Not every one learns in the same way or at the same pace. The attitudes, understandings, and practices of our families and communities affect our psychosexual development and involve all aspects of our selfhood and our relationships to others. The process will bring its share of fascination, frustration, anxiety, ambivalence, and strong convictions. We all have to learn which signals to heed—from the body, the heart, our parents, our peers, or the guidance of the Spirit. There aren't any easy answers, and we are not expected to reach maturity without passing through all the challenging stages of human development.

II: THE TEACHER

The Gospel of John offers us two sets of verses which should be a source of encouragement to every member of our class. Jesus reassures his followers: "I have said these things to you while I am still with you. But the Advocate, the Holy Spirit, whom the Father will send in my name, will teach you everything and remind you of all that I have said to you" (John 14:25–26 New Revised Standard Version [NRSV]). The Holy Spirit is not a cosmic police officer seeking to apprehend and condemn us for our faltering steps toward wholeness. The text speaks of the Spirit as our Advocate, as the one beside us to guide us into the way of abundant life. The Holy Spirit is a strong life coach, teaching us how to find and fulfill our destiny as individuals, families, and communities. For Christians, the deeper meaning of the words and deeds of Christ will be refreshed, refined, and renewed under the tutelage of the Spirit who dwells within us. The Spirit does not limit instructions to so-called religious matters alone. All areas of our lives are within the range of the Spirit's expertise and concern. Our sexuality is such a central and significant aspect of who we are, it would be unthinkable that the Spirit might be indifferent to this life-enriching aspect of our being. And what kind of teacher is the Holy Spirit? The answer is— dynamic, fully embracing, and engaged with us because the Spirit is ever-present to us and in us.

Encountered in the winds of change and the stirrings of our spirit, the Advocate will teach us everything—new knowledge for the living of all our days. Jesus continues, "I still have many things to say to you, but you cannot bear them now. When the Spirit of truth comes, he will guide you into all the truth; for he will not speak on his own, but will speak whatever he hears and he will declare to you the things that are to come" (John 16:12–13). In these verses, Jesus expresses two important truths. In the first place, his disciples, like us today, can only take in so much at a time. Sometimes, we need to absorb more deeply what we have already learned before we can take in something new. After absorbing and integrating new things, our hearts and minds are ready for more. Even important basic truths will have little meaning for us until an interest in the questions emerges in our experience and consciousness. Answers to unasked questions are rarely valued or remembered.

Second, Jesus knew that the story of our life in community

is forever being written; there are "things to come" that, in their unfolding, the Holy Spirit will open our eyes to see. The Holy Spirit instructs us not only through the words of a sacred text but also through the stirring of our hearts that calls us to broaden our compassion, through the prodding of our conscience that recognizes injustice, and through the encounters with others that open our eyes to new ways of seeing and being.

Like the good teachers we have all experienced, the Holy Spirit meets students—us—where we are. The Spirit respects our differences and discerns our unique gifts and our peculiar impediments to growth. The Spirit patiently awaits our readiness for learning and commits to walk with us all the way to the place of gracious illumination. Even though we are a class of extraordinarily diverse persons, the Spirit seeks to set a climate of mutual respect and hospitality. All the students impact the learning process through the spirit of their relatedness. In fact, the Spirit directs our continuing education and values our experiences so much that we are treated as teaching assistants. The class on sexuality is team-taught; all our experiences under the guidance of the Spirit can help us see the truth and cultivate the discipline and wisdom for living a good life for self and community.

III: THE SOURCES

Jesus has sent the Holy Spirit to be our teacher, and we are all teaching assistants. All well and good, but we also need sources to study that offer us a deeper understanding of human sexuality. These include the Bible, our experiences, the experiences of others, and the accumulated wisdom of the community.

The Bible: The Bible is a primary sourcebook for faith and values. But human sexuality is neither an elective course nor is it easy. We cannot just memorize a few pat answers or find CliffsNotes with standard answers; this is a critical thinking and feeling course. We will need to bring a host of approaches and insights to discern what is true and what applies in any given circumstance. We are expected to employ rigorous critical thinking, with the confidence that critical thinking is certainly not a sin but rather a requirement.

Biblical wisdom seeks to move us beyond the letter of the law to the Spirit the law seeks to reflect. We are not expected to memorize pages of rules and regulations formulated for specific circumstances in a particular historical setting, but rather to understand the overarching and underlying message of love. We are urged to apply the Golden Rule of doing unto others as we would have them do unto us in each new situation as it presents itself. The counsel we offer to others should reflect what we would be willing to accept if we were in a similar situation. By putting ourselves in the place of the other, we are more likely to be sensitive and fair and less rigid and judgmental.

In the debate about sexuality, some people claim that their position reflects a divine mandate set forth in the Bible. They assume the rules and regulations, principles and precepts they rely upon, are absolutely binding on all who profess to be faithful practitioners of God's will. Yet the Bible from which they derive their idea of "absolute laws" is not a book that captures the whole of divine wisdom for all times and places. We received a fixed order of books (canon) to be included in the Bible, a defined and limited collection of divinely inspired writings, captured at a particular moment in the history of God's people. Yet the Bible even in its development was not static. There is continuing illumination. The phrase used so often in Matthew 5 by Jesus was: "It has been said by those of old . . . but I say unto you. . . ." The beauty of the Bible is its pattern of addressing changing circumstances out of evolving wisdom rooted and grounded in fundamental truth. Jesus knew that each day and each generation, new winds of the Spirit would bring afresh God's word to the people, not limited to ancient words on a page but written by the Spirit on the hearts of God's people. For that very reason, Jesus promised his disciples that they must continue in the word and that the Holy Spirit would be their director of continuing education.

No time or season is able to perceive the full scope of divine intention. "Time makes ancient good uncouth."[2] At the same time, there is no time or place without witness to God's truth. An open and honest reading of the Bible makes very clear that times and seasons elicit changed understandings and practices. Some people get nervous just hearing ideas that conflict with their inherited values. Those who fear openness to change may find it comforting to know that major changes in moral outlook are not instantly achieved with the first thoughts brought on by new times and new approaches. Basic change in moral outlook is slow. For this reason, in this class, no one is asked to give instant endorsement to the ideas that are suggested.

Students accustomed to receiving instruction from a fixed, firm authority may find this class unsettling—the complex responsibility of helping to define what is right and wrong or appropriate and beneficial for the common good is a serious challenge. Just as the Bible both condemns and condones slavery and second-class status for women, the Christian community and members of other faith traditions have been led by the Spirit to see more deeply into God's will than past traditions had indicated. Yet we can take heart from those who came before us. They wrestled with the same difficulty of discovering what was called for by a new day. We are the beneficiaries of their courageous struggle toward a more excellent way to fulfill our destiny under God.

Recall, if you will, the controversy in Acts chapter 15. There, the new church community struggled with the question of circumcision. The "way it had always been" was that only circumcised boys and men were certified members of the community of the faithful. As the church reached out to Gentiles, the community had to decide if the old rules still applied across the board. They had to discuss the possibility of a more inclusive understanding of what it means to be part of the covenant community. The conflict was so intense that a general conference of the church had to be convened to resolve the issue. There was fierce debate. Representatives from all sides presented the best case they could. Appeal was made to scripture, tradition, and how the Spirit was moving among the Gentiles. After extensive wrangling over the issue, a conclusion was reached which reversed the requirement of circumcision for all men. The leader of the meeting announced, "I have reached the decision that we should not trouble those Gentiles who are turning to God" (Acts 15:19). In the written resolutions, they included this message: "For it has seemed good to the Holy Spirit and to us to impose on you no further burden than these essentials: that you abstain from what has been sacrificed to idols and from blood and from what is strangled and from fornication. If you keep yourselves from these, you will do well. Farewell" (Acts 15:28–29). Those who believed that circumcision should be required of all men must have felt that the church had lost its religion, but in the course of time the change became an accepted norm. The list of prohibitions they kept included a kosher restriction and the requirement that members avoid fornication (sexual relations outside of marriage). Christians no longer follow the dietary restrictions, and those who embrace the spirit of healthy adult sexuality outside marriage have challenged the judgment against fornication.

At stake in the current conversation about sexuality is the question about which items must remain on the list of forbidden practices. We struggle to maintain the integrity of the apostles, who made changes only after they had heard from differing points of view and felt they had discerned the guidance of the Holy Spirit. Such spiritual struggle and openness to difference will deliver us from both inflexible traditionalism and destructive self-indulgence. Whatever stand we take on these matters let us earnestly seek to be able to say with a good conscience, "It . . . seemed good to the Holy Spirit and to us."

As was the case in Acts 15, the dictionary reflects new understandings in its various editions over time. Consider this: a Webster's dictionary in 1961 notes that the word "sexuality" derives from the Latin word *sexus* from the base *secare* which means "to cut, divide." (We've certainly found that sexuality can be a divisive subject!) Sex, in the 1961 dictionary definition, meant:

1. Either of the two divisions of organisms distinguished as male or female
2. The character of being male or female—what distinguishes one from the other
3. Anything connected with sexual gratification or reproduction or the urge for these, especially the attraction of individuals of one sex for those of the other

That same edition of the dictionary defined "sex appeal" as "the physical attractiveness and personal charm that attract members of the opposite sex," and "sex hygiene" as "the branch of hygiene dealing with sex and sexual behavior as they relate to the welfare of both the individual and the community."

Compare those definitions with the 2005 edition of *Merriam-Webster's Collegiate Dictionary*, which defined "sex" as "either of the two major forms of individuals that occur in many species and that are distinguished respectively as female or male especially on the basis of their reproductive organs and structures." Sexual intercourse has two definitions: a) intercourse between a male and a female in which the penis is inserted into the vagina; b) intercourse between individuals involving genital contact other than insertion of the penis into the vagina.

These later editions show our society's changing norms

and understandings. The church will certainly not always follow societal changes but its witness must always responsibly address what is changing around us. The Bible speaks to policies in the past as well as to what is happening now— sometimes judging and sometimes setting free. The Holy Spirit assists us in determining our most compelling guiding principles, while not neglecting other perspectives that also seek to safeguard us against harm and distortion. Fruitful discussion of divisive issues will require us to understand how we and our opponents understand what kind of book the Bible is and how we interpret it with integrity. Progressive Christians read the Bible in light of biblical criticism and are open to interpretations informed by contemporary scientific understandings.

Our experience and the experience of others: In addition to the Bible, our experience is a required "text" for this course on human sexuality. More than any other aspect of our lives, our experience of sexuality is both intensely personal, private, and particular while also interpersonal, public, and a universal part of being human. We refract sexuality through our own experiences of pain or pleasure, delight or disappointment, and shame or self-confidence. We bear their imprint, as well as the influence of parents and partners, culture and companions, past and present, and hopes and dreams. All these dimensions affect what we believe, what we feel, how defensive we are when we talk about sex, and the extent to which we feel compelled to justify our own behavior.

As we grow into psychosexual maturity, we carry powerful memories that are manifested in our attitudes and behaviors. To enter dialogue about sexuality honestly, we have to have the courage to recognize the power of our own experiences. Unless we are conscious and accepting of our own experiences, we may become excessively and intrusively conscientious about enforcing rules for others in the hope that our strictness partially commutes the penalties for our past transgressions and serves to check the temptations toward future sins. People who are most vigilant about sexual violations may be communicating more than religious virtue. Their outrage about the sins of others alerts the angels to check for unresolved personal conflicts in the accuser.

This power of experience and memory became clear to me when I attended a charismatic conference at Duquesne University in Pittsburgh, Pennsylvania, back in the eighties.[3] The conference speaker was Ruth Carter Stapleton, an evangelist and the sister of President Jimmy Carter. She addressed the issue of the healing of memories. She explained that many of the difficulties in our adult relationships went back to hurtful experiences we had early in life. She asked us to remember if some significant person in our early lives had accused, abused, or misused us. In some cases, the person who injured us might have already passed away. Others who hurt us deeply may still be alive and in some instances still a part of our family or community. She continued, "The Spirit is able to heal those memories and set us free to love again without the inhibiting impact of past injury."

Following her talk, Stapleton led us in an exercise of the healing of memories. She told us to close our eyes and think back to the event that had hurt us. "Where did it happen? Who was there? Find the place where it happened. Do you see it? Are you there? Now, what happened? Go on and see it. Help is on the way. I know it hurt you then and it still hurts you now." I was surprised as the vast auditorium began to be filled with sounds of sobbing or deep groans, muffled because the pain was too heavy to be bellowed out. I, too, found myself weeping. Then she said, "I'm going to ask Jesus to come to you and put his arms around you and heal that pain." I joined the audible expressions of relief and gratitude and a general buzzing of joyful catharsis.

In a few minutes, she interrupted what had become loud shouts of "Thank you, God, thank you, Jesus, bless your holy name." She asked us to let the person who had hurt us enter the picture. "How do you feel about that person? It's all right if you are still bitter about what happened. How could they do such a thing?" A different sound came from the audience, a sobbing from a different place, and once more the evangelist interrupted with a surprising insight. "The person who hurt you would not have done that to you if in some way he or she had not also been injured, hurt, or mistreated or was functioning out of a defect not of his or her own making. He or she or they need a healing touch from Jesus just as you have received. Will you join Jesus and go over and offer forgiveness while Jesus also heals and forgives? Put your arms around Jesus and that person. Say these words if you can, 'I forgive you even as I also have been forgiven.' " Then after yet another, different wave of subdued, cautious, and gentle release, Stapleton asked us, "Now doesn't that feel better?" And I did feel like a heavy fog had been lifted from all of us and sunlight had broken through the clouds of dark memories. We closed the session singing "Praise God, praise God. Praise God, praise God," to the tune of *Amazing Grace*. And it had been an amazing experience of grace indeed.

After the session, one young man shared what had been long ago forgotten in his early childhood. His mother had found him expressing sexual interest in the girl who lived next door and scolded him. She put him in a dark closet. In his panic, he pulled the knob out of the door and felt helplessly trapped. In that auditorium, he had managed to forgive his mother because he had thought of her for the first time as a person who had experienced something as harsh as what she had inflicted on him. Maybe, he wondered, something negative had transpired between his mother and his father or even earlier in her life. Perhaps there was a memory of deep hurt in her that had never been healed, or she was desperately trying to stamp out the urges in her son that she knew could lead to hurtful and inappropriate behavior she herself had experienced as a girl.

All loving parents hope to see the best outcomes for their children. We would like to help our children avoid the pain and suffering we experienced along the way. What we teach them is designed to chart a better course than what we struggled through ourselves. But children must also have the freedom to find their own way. It can be hard to know how much punishment or restraint is beneficial. Parents must both promote freedom and impart the knowledge to make better choices. We must find the best form of expressing tender loving care for the lives entrusted in our care and discern what we must do and what we must allow our children to do for themselves. Hence, all parents must study hard, especially, in this part of the course on sexuality.

When we think of God as our heavenly parent, we are recognizing ourselves as children of God. What we have learned about God should suggest to us what God's response might be toward our sexual behavior. In the situations of our children breaking the rules or failing to conform to expectations, we must determine whether we will scold, blame, threaten, and reject our children or correct, instruct, restrain such action, and forgive them, so that blessings may flow from making better choices. I do not think God would put us in the closet and keep us there until we promised never to do it again.

As a parent, God does not reject us but rather corrects us. A woman was brought before Jesus by the religious authorities of the community, who had caught her in adultery. They were ready to stone her, but he stopped them, saying, "Let anyone among you who is without sin be the first to throw a stone at her" (John 8:7b). Jesus refused to punish her and instead told her she was free to go and live a new life.

Jesus reflected the spirit of our heavenly mother and father in his response. In Jesus's own Jewish tradition, adultery is clearly condemned. But he rejects using religion to stone a sinner. I am fully aware that in the Bible there are instructions to do some stoning—even a rebellious youth was to be stoned. The Spirit, however, has and can still overcome brutal rules that cause even more harm than the sin being condemned. To destroy persons because of sin is to destroy also the good in them and to deny the transforming power of the love of God. The God of love, mercy, and forgiveness (also from Jesus's Jewish tradition) is reflected in Jesus's actions. Jesus shows us in this story that the parental love of God works for our well-being through healing and forgiveness, not primarily through harsh punishment for our mistakes in living the gift of sexuality. God loves us where we are, as we are, and loves us into being all that we were ever meant to be.

My perspective on sexuality is the product of many complex forces, as it is for all of us: parental guidance, religious instruction, study in college and seminary, values of my community, biological development, my exploration of sexual expression, my delights and disappointments, and my continuing quest for maturity in my stewardship of the gift of sex. I am grateful for the many ways the Spirit has worked with me and helped me learn from my failures as well as my joys. I have learned that God, nature, and our bodies are more like positive advocates than hostile adversaries.

The wisdom of the community. In our most intense arguments about sex, many of us appeal to what God wills. However, if the truth be known, what we believe is also impacted by sociological factors as well. Even in the most deeply religious society, rules and regulations about human behavior bear marks of what the community feels is in its best interest. We may think that our arguments are strengthened when we claim that a practice is totally the mandate of God. We are closer to the truth when we acknowledge that the elders of the community, under the guidance of the Spirit, set forth the principles by which the community could survive and thrive. Usually religious traditions sanctify what the society considers necessary, even though perceived necessity changes from time to time. Things which were once condoned but proved to be harmful to the community are usually replaced. Child sacrifice, immolation, and stoning are just a few of the ways sin used to be punished, but no more. The Spirit can lead societies away from harm and toward closer understandings of God's loving will.

IV: THE CURRICULUM

This course in sexuality is just one part of our overall pursuit of a PhD—Praising and Honoring the Divine. But before we move too quickly to do that PhD, I suggest we turn our attention to the current controversy about sex: what it means to be human and what God wills for us as sexual human beings.

Human life is a gift from God and our sexuality is an aspect of that gift. Our bodies are not the disposable wrapping for our souls but are a part of the wholeness of the gift of life we have received from God. God's creation is good, and we are invited to celebrate the fullness of our lives, including our sexuality, as part of creation. To be alive is to grow, change, and struggle, as we experience successes, failures, and the whole journey of life from beginning to end. If we live well, we will come to broader understandings of the meaning of our sexuality through love's power to nurture our freedom and our responsibility.

God has made each of us unique. Although we are similar in many ways, there are countless ways in which we are different, including our sexuality. An unknowable mystery of being distinguishes each of us from the other—each person has a unique sexual blueprint that informs who we will become. The contours of our lives are developed in similar and dissimilar patterns. In many ways we are alike and in many ways we are different—and different does not mean deficient.

Life is conceived in relationship and our humanity is nurtured in the context of other caring persons. To be human is to be embedded in nature and human community and also in a larger spiritual wholeness of being. The experience of individuality may seem exclusively singular and private, but it is always only an aspect of multilayered existence in a larger community. We impact the communities in which we live, even as we are impacted by them. How we live our lives makes a difference in the lives of others, to a greater or lesser degree, and our family, friends, and communities help shape our sexual attitudes and behaviors.

The church of my youth was clear and uncompromising on two issues at the heart of the current controversy about sexuality. First, there were to be no sexual relations outside the bonds of marriage. Second, sexual relationships between persons of the same gender were strictly forbidden. Leaders searched the scriptures with a fine-toothed comb to make the case that premarital sex and same-gender lovemaking were outside the will of God. They accompanied their preaching and teaching about these matters with the threat of a hammer hanging over the heads of violators. Against any public report of such sins of perversion they launched impassioned sermons about Sodom and Gomorrah or unnatural affections leading to a reprobate mind and being banished to the hottest region of hell.

In the eyes of these church leaders, these sexual offenses were such an abomination in the sight of God that the church was called to strike preemptively against such transgressions and to foment fear in the hearts of young people. Shaming was a major instrument to drive the point home. Once they apprehended the offenders, they loaded them with guilt, and the offenders became official object lessons for divine retribution and community sanctions. For example, they publicly exposed any woman who had a child out of wedlock, and they sentenced her to silence and denied her communion until the time of punishment was completed. Interestingly enough, the male partner to such pregnancies was never publicly sanctioned.

Leaders used a colorful lexicon of names to rail against offenders and to drive them underground: "dykes," "sissies," and "queers." Yet they also tolerated suspect members if they did not "flout" their behavior or seek to "pollute" other young people in the church. Volunteer workers, talented musicians, or compassionate helpers of the poor or elderly were granted a place in the church family if they could endure hearing about the wrath of God regularly launched against them like grenades from the pulpit.

For the second half of my ministerial years, I have served in progressive circles where a different set of values prevail. I taught at a progressive seminary and then became the pastor of an open and affirming congregation, The Riverside

Church in New York City, after a long and intense grappling with the issue of sexuality under the leadership of my predecessor, William Sloane Coffin, voted on June 2, 1985, to affirm what is called A Statement of Openness, Inclusion, and Affirmation. It condemned all acts of harassment, exclusion, violence, and intimidation based on homophobia; sought to address homophobia in the church; created programs about sexuality; and welcomed gay and lesbian persons as full equals in Christ. The statement represents the spirit emerging in other congregations at the time, a spirit now found in increasing numbers of congregations. The church seeks to guide individuals in greater freedom and responsibility to decide when and under what circumstances they would become sexually active. Such sexual freedom was so accepted that a friend of mine once asked, "What behavior *would* be considered a sin at this church?" My answer to her was that it probably would be considered a sin to try to make a list of sins by which to judge other people. Of course this is an exaggeration, but not by far. Progressive churches are more likely to err in defining what a communal sense of values would include than drawing up a list of sins. They emphasize following Jesus's example of being more ready to include than to exclude.

As I lived and served on both sides of the sexual divide— conservative and progressive—I felt the Spirit leading me to greater understanding. Each side has important ideas to contribute to the course on sexuality. The power of sexual energy is like the power of love; it calls us to freedom ("Perfect love casts out fear" 1 John 4:18) and at the same time its mature fulfillment requires responsibility. It is an energy which, if not regulated, can become the ruling power in our lives. It will seize us obsessively and be so demanding that what is only a part of life takes over the rightful place of other aspects. Thus, powerful enrichment can become powerful enslavement and idolatry. Hence the conservative effort to encourage constraints and regulatory principles is a valuable consideration in helping adolescents reach psychosexual maturity.

Still, the imperative of abundant life requires us to celebrate freedom, which is necessary for love. Sexuality bound by narrow rules, regulations, and restraints suffocates the individuality, creativity, and the mutual respect and vulnerability which the Spirit of love seeks to nourish. Fixation on external demands can stunt the growth of the heart. It seeks to express its own truth and discover the hidden delights of a voyage into the unknown. The progressive impulse is to move us beyond our servitude to inherited conventionalities and set us free to hear what the Spirit is saying to us today. Let us remember that our divine director of continuing education leads us through new challenges presented by changes in our world. The Spirit calls on us to upgrade our understandings through our study together.

The Bible offers us fundamental values that do not lock us into every detail of particular biblical passages written to that past time and place. Not every man will have to be circumcised. Masturbation will not deny anyone a seat at the messianic banquet. Those who are not virgins as they stand at the matrimonial altar need to know that God brings a generous measure of mercy and grace to all weddings.

In New Testament times there was no concept of what

we now speak of as homosexuality. There were instances of same sex relationships but they were not thought to be normal expressions rooted in the unique sexual orientation of persons. Now we know more. We understand that a person's sexual orientation is not simply a matter of choice. It is now clearer that whether one is gay or straight usually has a genetic basis. The old assumption was that everybody was heterosexual, and if some behaved differently, they were perverse. Now we know that it would be perversion for homosexual persons to force themselves into heterosexual relationships that are not true to who they are. We should not assume as we have generally done, that God intends every person to be straight. God has a purpose for creating diversity as a feature of human life. And God has compassion, especially, for the despised and rejected. Treating badly those who are different from ourselves offends God far more than our using the name of God to condemn those who can not fulfill traditional models of sexual expression.

Our sexual orientation is a gift of God's creativity. How we achieve sexual maturity is both a communal and personal responsibility. We are now discovering that identifying when a person is ready for adult sexual relations is not just a matter of whether they have a signed marriage license. Readiness has to do with a person's genuine love for the other, self-acceptance and self-understanding, and the ability to show mutual respect and care for one's mate. Readiness is linked to one's willingness to be trusting and vulnerable, a strong commitment to stand by one's partner under the stresses and strains of modern life. It also includes the ability and willingness to take responsibility for the fruit of the relationship—

not just sexual satisfaction but a commitment to share fully in the life and death issues that flow from such relationships.

These principles serve as a challenging standard for all couples, married or single. The biblical call for marriage envisions such factors, but the Spirit also keeps us moving. The Spirit is calling for enrichment and refinement of our understanding of marriage. What will promote solid family values for people who approach life out of a faith perspective?

I would like to see a coming together of perspectives that honor both the traditional values of fidelity, commitment, and responsibility and the mature progressive understanding that challenges society to embrace more inclusive values that reflect the fresh winds of the Spirit. Together, we must lift up these values of responsibility and inclusiveness so that people will know whether or not that they are ready for marriage or for sexual intimacy. It is time to create a standard for individuals to gauge their readiness for the intimacy which marriage requires. Just as a bridal magazine has checklists and guidelines for planning a ceremony and selecting what kind of dress to wear, religious communities must offer a checklist and guidelines that show how to be ready for the intimacy and responsibility of marriage.

When we use such a term as family values, we must ask, what kind of parent is our God? This might be the most important question on our final exam, the key to everything we understand about sexuality. The answer we give will inevitably reflect our own personalities, but we also need to understand the attributes of God as revealed in Jesus Christ. People often describe God in their own image. However,

God as found in the life of Jesus Christ is a Divine Parent who loves us beyond consideration of our virtues and our vices.

God wills us to be in community under the conditions of freedom. God knows us better than we know ourselves and respects our differences. We are encouraged to "keep our hearts with all diligence," (Proverbs 4:23) because out of the heart flows guidance for the crucial issues of life. External compliance with imposed guidelines without the heart's commitment falls short of God's will. Remember once again the words of my father that in the University of Grace not all the students will make an A. In regards to sexuality, it is unlikely that any of us will get a passing grade, unless God is grading on a curve. We read in the confessions of Psalm 51 that even King David could fail miserably, according to the most liberal standards. He was nevertheless a person of God's own heart, as are we all.

And what does God will for us as family values? God desires truth in the inward parts. The fruits of that truth will be joy, peace, abundant life, sharing, caring, justice, love, and acceptance. Without an inward truth that honors all humanity as created by God, we cannot experience the fullness of life that God intends for each of us.

Christians must take a fresh look at what we preach and teach about sex. We must seek a better balance between freedom and responsibility. We all can be learners and teachers together in the lifelong course in sexuality. To enrich family life through deepening love in marriage requires both liberals and conservatives to work on readiness for marital sexual relations. We must take a position that will increase a sense of responsibility and reduce unnecessary hypocrisy, self-deception, dishonesty, and guilt. I am strongly committed to following Paul's admonition, "For the letter kills but the Spirit gives life" (2 Corinthians 3:6). Let us listen to the wisdom of the Spirit and of each other about God's love for our gay and lesbian brothers and sisters. God, our heavenly Parent, Mother and Father of us all, wishes for all the beloved children of the family to enjoy the rights, privileges, responsibilities, and delights of mature sexual expression.

Gender Equality:
For God's Sake and Ours

We all remember the playground retort, "Sticks and stones may break my bones, but words will never hurt me." Most of us have come to realize the absurdity of that statement, despite the bravado with which it was typically uttered. Words have power—the power to harm or help, uphold or put down. Can you recall a time you were called a derogatory name, one that meant to demean you because of your race, ethnicity, gender, sexual orientation, income, appearance, intelligence, or family circumstances? Now, can you remember a time you were called a name that affirmed some aspect of your being? Names are perhaps the most powerful of words—they speak to identity, impacting our sense of self and perceptions of others; they reflect our most intimate sense of how we see ourselves and how others see us. Words matter. Names matter.

For an example, biblical scholarship identifies two creation narratives: Genesis 1:1–2:3 and Genesis 2:4–25. In Genesis 2, Adam—translated "man"—whom God created from the dust of the ground is given the power to name every living creature and finally to declare of the one formed from his rib, "This one shall be called Woman, for out of Man this one was taken" (Genesis 2:23b, NRSV). By contrast, in the earlier biblical account of creation in Genesis 1, God declares, " 'Let us make humankind in our image, according to our likeness.' . . . So God created humankind in his image, in the image of God he created them, male and female he created them," and to them God gave the shared responsibility of dominion over creation.

For centuries upon centuries, church history and societal practice ignored the Genesis 1 account of men and women made equally in the image of God. Instead Genesis 2 was used because it reinforced patriarchal assumptions that men should have the power to name, define, and dominate all of creation—including women (even if a careful and critical reading of the text doesn't support that popular interpretation).

As the modern day "women's liberation movement" was developing in the sixties and seventies, women in the church were looking anew at patriarchal language and customs so long-standing and normative that many had not even noticed or questioned them before. In the late 1970s and 1980s, in response to feminists in the church, many progressive Christian churches and denominations began to change their worship language to "inclusive language." Many women in churches (and some men too) decided that masculine words like "man," "mankind," "he," and "his," which had claimed to include women. In fact, these words reinforced the idea that women were subordinate to men and implied maleness was the norm, with femaleness as the aberration or exception. This was called sexist language. Masculine words called up male images in people's imaginations, rendering women invisible, and reinforced male domination over women in the church.

It was not only masculine language about *people* that began to feel exclusive or sexist, but also language about God. The critics of male gender bias applied the same standard of inclusive language to God-talk. The predominantly masculine terminology for God (the few feminine metaphors and references notwithstanding) fostered the belief that God's being and nature were intricately and exclusively tied to maleness. Some who were willing to accept more inclusive changes to language about humankind felt that it went too far, might even be blasphemous, to try to change the way we talk about God. How could the Bible, tradition, and the church of their childhood be wrong? To some, inclusive language seemed unnatural, unfaithful, and unnecessary.

Not incidental to the problem is the fact that, at that time, the ones doing most of the public talking and writing about God and God's people were male. With a few exceptions in the seventies, the clergy were almost exclusively male, and that male domination extended through all levels of church leadership and scholarship. God was generally referred to as "He," "King," or "Our Dear Heavenly Father."

Exclusive, male-biased language confronted worshippers at every turn—in the spoken words of sermons and prayers, in translations of the Bible, in hymnals, in orders of worship, and in common books of prayer. It was not that these terms were wrong, but the exclusive use of male names and images suggested that God was more identified with men than women. Since we know that God is a spirit, it should be obvious that God is not limited to male or female. The action to change the imbalance was to insert female language, exclude male terms, alternate between the use of male and female references, or to find ways around the use of any male or female names or imagery when speaking of God. Women's power to change language had clear limits. For example, they couldn't demand a preacher speak inclusively, though they might ask. In other instances, they created improvised solutions to the change they sought. Some churches, in the absence of an inclusive version of hymns, put a notice every week in the bulletin, encouraging people to change words as they sang them. Others provided a folder that told worshippers how to substitute inclusive words in litanies and hymns. I know of at least one case where a group of women in the church spent days going through the hymnals together, crossing out the sexist language and writing in the inclusive words. Not every member was pleased with the marked-up hymnals, and, in many churches, there were those who bristled at these changes to their beloved old familiar prayers, liturgies, and hymns. Nonetheless, women and others who wanted change persisted, and denominations published new, inclusive hymnals in the 1980s and 1990s.

It was also not too long before denominations had a more inclusive language translation of the Bible, the New Revised Standard Version, which many churches use now. The result of long and painstaking translation by biblical scholars working under the aegis of the National Council of the Churches of Christ in the USA, the New Revised Standard Version translation replaced masculine words about humanity, either returning to the original Hebrew or Greek for accurate and more inclusive translations (e.g., "mortal" or "humankind" for "man"), or in other places inserting references to women (adding "sisters" to read "brothers and sisters," for instance), or substituting a related word (e.g., using "kindred" instead of "brothers"), making note of the addition or substitution in a footnote. It should be noted, however, that the New Revised Standard Version does not use fully inclusive language for God, retaining, for instance, "He" and "His" in reference to the divine.

In the wake of the ardent efforts of inclusive language advocates these past forty years or so, inclusive language has come to seem more "normal." Many churches take these things for granted now, with their more inclusive hymnals and Bibles. Their leaders do not make a big deal about saying he or she, his or hers, sons and daughters, sisters and brothers, Mother and Father God, and brotherhood and sisterhood. Some seminaries make it an explicit requirement that students preparing for ministry use inclusive language in their papers and on tests. Even though at times it is awkward to do so, I avoid the use of male language or I seek to balance between God as Father and Mother. Exclusive use of male images conveys the false impression that God is more like a man. Because God is a spirit and has no biological gender, we are closer to the truth when we avoid any suggestion that we really think of God as more male than female. By varying our usage we acknowledge that our terminology is a reflection of human convenience and not a precise theological declaration about the nature of God. People of faith should be prepared to answer the question, is there any theological reason why God may not be referred to as "She" or "He"?

Progress has not, however, been steady. Breaking years of training and unconscious habits is hard. In addition, different ethnic churches from African American churches to new churches comprised of immigrants from Asia, Latin America, Africa, and the Middle East carry forward older terms that have a different history in their communities than in predominantly white churches. For example, calling God or Jesus "Lord" has been a subtle way of saying a slave owner or oppressive government was not lord. Seeing how "Lord" also reinforces male power over women requires admitting that oppression might exist, even in a community with a mission to end oppression.

Recognizing and advocating the end of male oppression of women must become as intentional as our efforts to insure homeland security against terrorists. Staggering is the reality that while one soldier was dying in battle in Iraq each day, three women were being murdered here in the United States by men, most of whom were husbands or intimate partners of their victims.

People report now that some churches which embraced inclusive language are backing away from it. Leaders in worship seem less conscientious about making their language include women and men together and using both female and male images for God. New generations are filling the pews who never knew there was a battle over inclusive language and thus have no deep commitment to holding a line they don't realize may be lost. They are likely to inherit gender biases from the Bible and our culture without being sensitized to the serious theological error and the negative consequences of such an understanding.

Yes, some churches call Jesus the only begotten child. Still, some people—those who were never convinced in the early battle of the sixties and seventies, and those who weren't even born while that battle raged and are considering this for the first time—want to know, why don't we call Jesus "son"? Wasn't he a man? Some call God "the sovereign one." Why don't we say, "Lord"? Didn't Jesus call God "Lord"? Yes, but there's a problem with *only* using male terms for God—it tends to work in reverse to make "male" into God. That certainly makes "female" far less than equal. A two-thousand-year tradition of sexism is probably not going be reversed in just forty short years, but we would do well to speak as truthfully as possible when we speak of God, whom we worship and serve.

The changes in language and worship have not been taken seriously enough. Too many people saw them as cosmetic and did not take the problem of sexism seriously enough, despite the fact that some denominations went even further. In the late 1970s, they not only changed worship language, but they also tried to open doors for women to lead churches, insisting that searches for senior pastors include women as candidates. More and more women entered seminaries as students, not as spouses of students. A decade later, some seminaries had a majority of women students, but ordained women still found a stained-glass ceiling. Denominations with bishops who appoint pastors had put some women in senior pulpits, but in denominations that allow local churches to call their own ministers, the women in senior pulpits are still few, too few.

A woman I know quit a job at a very successful financial

institution with a salary well into six digits. She wanted to become a preacher and graduated from seminary to pursue her dream. She began to despair because everywhere she tried to get a church, she felt the search committee was only looking at her because the rules said they should. She was sure no church was ever going to call her to lead it. She is among many talented women still waiting for a pulpit that will allow them to live out their calls to ministry and use all their skills.

The resistance to change reminds me of the story of this little boy who could not get his grammar straight. He kept saying, "I have went." His frustrated teacher made him write one hundred times on the blackboard, "I have gone. I have gone." When he finished, the teacher was not in the room, so he wrote a note, "I have finished my assignment and I have went home."

Churches' concessions may have been made to appease women so as to avoid conflicts. I have observed in the church that we might work to be inclusive in scriptures, in hymns, in prayers, and even in announcements, but our deeper problem is that we are not fully committed to the idea that women and men are equally made in the image of God. Many of us have not been sure that inclusive language was mandated by the gospel. Some Christians still suspect that criticism of sexism is just a secular feminist critique designed to destroy the church. We may have hoped that, after the women finished protesting, this political movement would fail, and we could go on with business as usual. Others thought, "Yes, I'm for women, but the National Organization of Women might come on a little too strong for some folk." Still others may have even been suspicious of the World Council of Churches Ecumenical Decade of Churches in Solidarity with Women, started in 1988. The World Council wanted to assure that women would be represented in their top leadership, that women would be on delegations to their various assemblies and conferences, and that women's roles in the church and the world would not be characterized by abuse, harassment, or second-class citizenship. They wanted to encourage churches to bear witness to a hope that every girl and boy would have every opportunity to become all they were ever meant to be.

Even with the slow rate of change, developing inclusive language and making room for women's leadership in the church has been easier than changing how we speak of and think about God. For many Christians, it seems natural to call God "Father" because Jesus said, "When you pray, say, Our Father who art in heaven." When Jesus was on the cross, he cried out, "Father, forgive them. They know not what they do." Paul, in Romans 8:15, reminded us that we "cry *Abba*, Father." For many, calling God "Father" is our witness that we are children of God. In the noninclusive version we sang, "This is my Father's world." It seems very natural to many to exclusively continue to call God "Father."

Why debate the name of God? Why not, instead, get on with the business of creating a just society where all God's children are respected and protected, encouraged and supported? Some church members still insist that there is work to be done without having to worry about what we call God. Why not? Because what we call God matters a great deal. If we only call God "Father," we perpetuate the problems of idolatry and patriarchy and the larger problem of societal norms and behaviors towards women. Just as racism involves the idolatrous elevation of one race or ethnicity above all others in significance and value, the same can be the result of exclusively conceiving of God as male. When we only conceive of God as male, we limit God and we assign divinized status to males. As with all "isms," sexism has the capacity to separate us from God, from each other, and from our own true and best selves. Scripture warns us time and again that we must deny ourselves any specificity of identity that becomes an occasion for the diminishment of others or that separates us from God. That egocentrism is challenged everywhere in the Bible.

Patriarchy has a number of dimensions. It elevates maleness as closer to divinity; it reinforces men dominating women; and it denies women equal dignity and respect. Male dominance wastes women's gifts by proscribing and prescribing who and what they can do with their lives, with the primary focus on serving the needs of men or their families. In its worst forms, male domination over women fosters abuse, exploitation, and hatred of women. All of these dimensions of patriarchy result in an unequal distribution of power, honor, and respect along gender lines, so that job opportunities are limited for women and result in differential remuneration for the same work done. Women are also excluded from certain roles and responsibilities, even in the church. They are always enthusiastically welcomed as members of the support team but are less frequently given the opportunity to provide top leadership and authority.

The elevation of the male goes hand in hand with the downgrading of the female. The identification of maleness with God means feminine characteristics are associated with weakness and masculine traits with strength. Even worse, interpretations of Genesis 3 blame women for being the source of evil and sin in the world and insist that men are victims of women's seductions. People say, "Remember, now. Jesus appointed only men as disciples and not women." They quote Paul's letter to Timothy, "I permit no woman to teach or to have authority over a man; she is to keep silent" (1 Timothy 2:12). The Hebrew Scriptures repeatedly declare, "I am the God of Abraham, Isaac, and Jacob" with less frequent mentioning of Sarah, Hagar, Rebecca, Rachel, or any of the other women. According to those who use the Bible to support and sustain patriarchy, women are supposed to live under subjection to men, who are considered to be morally and spiritually superior.

While feminists urge women to rise up, challenge traditional stereotypes, and take on the rights and responsibilities granted to men, the pro-patriarchy factions of the church say we must remember that the place of the woman is in the home. They say we must look at the physiological differences between men and women. The muscle strength of the man should justify that superiority. Women are the weaker sex.

Instead of seeing the oppression of women as a grave injustice in the church and in society, many take umbrage and talk about the battle of the sexes. Men and women are pitted against one another as competitors, as if men should not care about women as equal human beings, as if men will

lose if justice prevails. Instead of working to make sure
women are not dehumanized and oppressed, they try to rob
women of their freedom through harassment, legislation
against their own bodily integrity, or threats of violence,
abandonment, or other harm.

Such ideas, based on prejudices, do not reflect the whole
truth from the Bible, history, or science. The Bible depicts
many strong women leaders and heroes. In Exodus, Moses's
sister Miriam helps save the lives of her people. She is herself
a prophet and leader. In the book of Judges, Deborah was a
great leader of men. Ruth and Naomi preserved for us the
line that led to King David, and out of that lineage, Jesus
Christ himself, through his father Joseph. We know that
Jesus was close to many women who were supportive members of his community, and the Samaritan woman was the
first evangelist. She affirmed the Messiahship of Jesus and
invited her community to come and see Him. Women were
the first to witness the empty tomb and the ones to get the
word of the resurrection out to the disciples. Christian
redemption and the church itself could not have happened
without the intelligence, leadership, and actions of strong
women. In fact, because the words in Hebrew and Greek for
both Spirit and Wisdom are feminine, it is possible to see that
God can be seen as feminine.

We can not only refocus on the often overlooked women
in the Bible, but we can also take a fresh and critical look at
the texts that are often misused and misunderstood. We
know that the Bible, including the most sexist passages or
those most frequently used to uphold the subjugation of

women, came out of and reflected a particular social, historical, and ecclesiastical context two thousand years ago. The
later epistles attributed to Paul, sometimes referred to as the
"disputed epistles," are now considered to reflect not only
different authorship but also different social structures than
the first-century church, developing Christian teachings to
support a more rigidly hierarchical and patriarchal social
structure than the more egalitarian and mutual one upheld
in the earlier Pauline letters and in Jesus's own teaching.

Rosemary Radford Ruether, in *Sexism and God-Talk:
Toward a Feminist Theology*,[1] sums it up well: "There is no
question that patriarchy is the social context for both the Old
and the New Testament and that this social context has been
incorporated into religious ideology on many levels. Nevertheless both Testaments contain resources for the critique of
patriarchy and of the religious sanctification of patriarchy."
Ruether identifies some of the resources and themes for that
critique of patriarchy:

> Four themes are essential to the prophetic-liberating
> tradition of Biblical faith: 1) God's defense and vindi-
> cation of the oppressed; 2) the critique of the domi-
> nant system of power and their power holders; 3) the
> vision of a new age to come in which the present sys-
> tem of injustice is overcome and God's intended
> reign of peace and justice is installed in history; and
> 4) finally, the critique of ideology, or of religion, since
> ideology in this context is primarily religious.
> Prophetic faith denounces religious ideologies and

systems that function to justify and sanctify the dominant, unjust social order. These traditions are central to the Prophets and to the mission of Jesus. Hence, the critical-liberating tradition is the axis around which the prophetic-messianic line of Biblical faith revolves as a foundation for Christianity.[2]

At best, with the most difficult texts that would seem to justify women's subordination, we can look critically at the social, historical circumstances of their writing, measuring them against the overarching message of scripture and life and the words of Jesus, and hold on to what is consistent with the biblical ethic of justice and compassion, while setting aside that which contradicts the liberating love of God made known in Jesus Christ. Consider Galatians, one of the "undisputed epistles," attributed to Paul without challenge. Paul writes, "In Christ Jesus you are all children of God through faith. As many of you as were baptized into Christ have clothed yourselves with Christ. There is no longer Jew or Greek, there is no longer slave or free, there is no longer male and female: for all of you are one in Christ Jesus" (Galatians 3:28). At the end of the day, there is no way to avoid making a choice as we encounter troubling cultural norms reflected in biblical literature. We who consider ourselves progressive have to decide if we are open, by the Spirit, to hear the deeper message of scripture and let go of a particular cultural or historical moment captured in time; we will either bind ourselves to cultural norms or seek eternal verities at work.

Peter J. Gomes, dean of Memorial Church at Harvard

University, encourages us to read the Bible with mind and heart. In his book *The Good Book* there is a chapter on "The Bible and Women: The Conflicts of Inclusion," in which he reviews the scriptures, which have been used for and against the equality of women.[3] He summarizes his position by appealing to an article written by Malcolm D. Tolbert that appeared in *The New Has Come: Emerging Roles among Southern Baptist Women*:

> Tolbert writes, "I do not understand the pattern of male dominance reflected in the Bible as an expression of the will of God. It is rather the reflection of the culture in which Jews and Christians as well as pagans lived. I am governed rather by the insights found in various key texts which make it possible for Christians to criticize the structures of society and the Church. These passages, Mark 10:43 and Galatians 3:28 emphasize the ideals of servanthood and mutuality in relationships rather than the ascendency of any one person or group of persons over others." He is of a large and growing company.[4]

WHERE DO WE GO FROM HERE?

It is time for the rebirth or renewal of the church like that first birth at Pentecost, when our ways of speaking about humanity and our language for God are no longer a stumbling block. Embracing the full equality of women will unleash the power of the Spirit, and we will be able to understand each other better and discover a new unity of faith and purpose. Yes, in the fullness of a new day, let's look for the promise God declares that "I will pour out my Spirit upon all flesh, and your sons and your daughters shall prophesy" (Acts 2:17b). If we are open to the Spirit we will find ourselves moving beyond former conditions and into a glorious democratization. For intelligence, courage, leadership, and perseverance against oppression can come in any size, color, gender, and shape.

The evidence of women made equally in the image of God is in the Bible and our history, so we Christians have a job before us. We have to make up our minds as to where we stand. We have to decide that we will not be carriers of attitudes, policies, and actions that perpetuate the dehumanization and oppression of women. Women who have experienced this oppression know that our language, our very understandings of scripture, tradition, and even of God reinforce this injustice. They have thrown down the penalty flag. They have blown the whistle, indicating foul play: sexist problems are so buried in our language and practices that, without even thinking about it, we perpetuate them.

Though some in our society may still want to label feminine as inferior to masculine, Christian faith must be better. Christians must base our understandings of gender not on the social institutions of patriarchy but on a common humanity, both male and female, created in God's own image. Women have not only rocked the cradle, they have also sparked revolutionary movements, and they have made contributions to every category of excellence in civilization. If Christian faith denies this equality of women and men, it denies the basic truth of creation.

If we begin with this egalitarian understanding of gender, we have to say that God cares about the language we use to refer to each other and to speak of divinity. If we use only male language—He, King, or Father—to name God, these affect our encounter with God and our thinking and our behavior, and they limit our full experience of God. Male dominance and female subordination are sinful distortions, caused by the Fall, as in the account of Genesis where the new human beings disobeyed and forfeited the benefits of remaining in the Garden of Eden, and certainly was not God's original intention for human relationships. Christian faith calls women and men to join together to overcome domination and subordination. We must learn to name and praise God in ways that do not make an idol of masculinity or femininity. We need more freeing language, truer to the many dimensions and experiences of God disclosed by Jesus, who, in his parables and stories, depicted God as both feminine and masculine. If we cannot call God "Mother," neither can we call God "Father," for female is as much a window on divinity as male.

Some people will claim that God is mystery and that we should not try to put human limitations on God. But I have noticed that this problem of limitations does not come up when God is referred to as "Father," which is also a specific and limiting word. The critics' assumption here is that God in female language limits divinity, whereas God in male terms does not. Even though the mystery of divine reality defies precise definition, we can access experiences of God through the language we use and build a bridge into the mysteries we do not yet fully apprehend. These mysteries touch us, and we share them together through the words we use in worship. Any bridges we build from mystery to worship must strive to grasp as fully as possible that vast, unfathomable reality we call "God."

The heart of Christianity resides in the feelings, the acts, and the experiences of our communities and how they stand in relationship to the divine. Does God want to be called "Mother"? Who is God in whom we live and move and have our being? We can call a name. What name? Is God better understood and addressed as Earth, Wind, Water, or Fire? Is God Ocean, Space, or Void? Or Sister, Brother, Friend? The Bible calls God many names. When we think about how vast life is and about how rich our experiences of life and its power are, we are made aware of the ways we may try to limit God. What we call God in worship is not just about our personal private God. Most of us would not even respect a God we made just for ourselves, just for our convenience. Our speaking of God must carry meaning for the whole people of God.

We must remember that God loves every race, nationality, religion, age, sex, sexuality, temperament, and ability, and each can reflect divinity. While our first understandings of God come from our parents, from our church, from the Bible, from the prophets, and from others, we mature in faith as our understanding expands to embrace the whole of God's creation. The women of the church have offered us a great gift in asking us to think beyond our limited patriarchal understandings of God. They have said, "Listen friends, in the Bible God is not only called 'Father.' There are images of God that represent God as a mother, others as midwife, some as mistress or sister." The Bible contains many images, though we too often just end up calling God "He."

God does not have an identity crisis; we do. God is spirit and is not nearly as worried about what we say as who we are. Jesus reminded his disciples that they will come on the last day saying, " 'Lord, Lord' and I will say, depart from me. I don't even know you, though you call me by the right name, your actions have not been pleasing in the sight of God" (Matthew 7:22 NRSV). The issue for Christians is not so much the name we say as what the name says about our values and commitments. God is not sitting around waiting to hear the exact "right" words. The right words flow from the right relationships, from our love and respect for each other and for creation. God cares about relationships that lead us to justice and righteousness. God cares deeply about our sensitivity to the cries of our sisters and our brothers more so than the perfection of our nomenclature.

When we think about what we call God, we must say, "If calling God 'Father' exclusively leads to the impression that maleness is more divine or more valuable than femaleness then we must never ever call God 'Father' again." When God the Father leads us to oppress women, rob them of their spirit and their bodies, subjugate them to a second-class place in the world, we must cease to call God "Father." If we name God "Father" so that we can abuse and oppress, exploit and exclude, discriminate and intimidate, ostracize, marginalize, stigmatize, and demonize women, we have made an evil idol of masculinity. We have not spoken to God, but to that idol. Our language cannot be used to justify that kind of behavior. It is as reprehensible as insisting that God is white in a racist society. By the same token, if calling God "Mother" exclusively would lead to a justification for the negation of all males and the demonization of the masculine, we have the same idolatry. For God is more truly named by what we do than by what we say.

When Moses stood before the burning bush and asked: "God if I accept your calling to be a liberator, who shall I say sent me? They are going to ask me, 'What is the name of the one who sent you?' " God said to Moses, "Moses, tell them, if they want to know my name, tell them my name is I Am Who I Am. And tell them that I Am has sent you to set the people free" (Exodus 3:13–14 NRSV). In taking up the same question from Moses, we must ask, "Who is this God who calls to us?" The I Am for us today might say, "I Am will be unto you whatever love demands, whatever names that set you free from your bondage and toward ways of life that are liberating and enriching for all." I Am can be Mother, Father, Friend, Sister, Brother, whatever sustains us in the responsibilities of love and of knowing ourselves as beloved of God. "I am your lover!" said God. We should worry less about whether our language limps along and more about getting our stride right. For God is constantly calling us, each by our own name, to walk toward the promised land, the place of grace and peace with each other.

In the church where I was raised, women held prominent places of leadership. There were always more women than men in the membership and their support was essential for any activity to be a success. I remember certain names of women who significantly impacted the life of my church: Mother Bennett, Mother Delk, B. Lewis Jones, Mattie B.

Cummings, The Rev. Ella Yarborough, Evangelist Bessie Smith, Mother Ethel Tatnall, and Bishop Ruby Woodson, to name a few.

Even in those days, pockets of membership resisted such inclusion. The most intense opposition said equality for women would be an abomination in the sight of God. I never could understand whether the attitude toward women in ministry was a male ego problem or deep theological conviction—the two often worked in tandem. But I always felt that there was rejoicing in heaven each time barriers fell and women could proudly say yes to the call of the spirit.

One of my profound satisfactions of being a seminary professor was exposure to the rich gifts of women preparing themselves for a call they had heard, even when their congregations were not yet ready to affirm their ministries. I have watched many of them move into ministerial roles and responsibilities. They serve with such distinction that hearts and minds are changed from resistance to enthusiastic endorsement of women in ministry.

In June of 2002, I had the sublime delight of introducing the Rev. Dr. Susan Johnson Cook as the first woman to be elected president of the ten-thousand member Hampton (Virginia) University Ministers' Conference. In 1983, she had been elected the first black woman to be a senior pastor in the two-hundred-year history of American Baptist Churches USA. Her other firsts include the first woman appointed chaplain of the New York City Police Department and the first female Baptist minister to receive a White House fellowship. The evening I introduced her in Hampton, I reminded the audience that in 1981, my asking Susan, a woman minister, to read the scripture and then inviting all women ministers to stand to be acknowledged had never been done at the conference before. I performed that revolutionary act to dramatize the scripture:

"In the last days it will be, God declares, that I will pour out my spirit up on all flesh, and your sons and your daughter shall prophesy, and your young men shall see visions, and your old men shall dream dreams" (Acts 2:17 NRSV).

Twenty-one years after I had asked the gathering how we could have the audacity to block the ministries of those who have been anointed by the same Spirit into our noble vocation, Dr. Susan Johnson Cook had become the president of the conference. The conference now gladly welcomes women and men to serve the conference so that the Spirit of God is free to treat us all the same without regard to gender.

3

Which Gospel Do You Believe About Race?

In the fall of 2008, I received a book titled *A Life Is More Than a Moment*. This book of photographs by Will Counts and essays by Will Campbell, Ernest Dumas, and Robert S. McCord recounts the 1957 desegregation of Central High School in Little Rock, Arkansas. Nine black students had risked their lives to break the color barrier. The book jacket carries a picture which became famous as a reflection of the tensions of the times.

A young black student named Elizabeth Eckford walks alone after being turned away from the school; she is followed by an angry crowd of whites. In the crowd is a young white student whose mother brought her to the anti-integration march. The angry scowl on the face of the white student captures the depth of racist bitterness and resentment at the heart of resistance to the Supreme Court order to end segregation.

The book contains other photographs of the same two students, one black, one white, taken forty years later. In these pictures, they are friends. They had worked through the painful memories of the mobs and the marches in 1957, when Governor Orval Faubus blocked the doors of Central

High. In 1997, Central High observed the fortieth anniversary of the desegregation of the school. At the commemoration, another former governor of Arkansas, who became the
forty-second president of the United States, Bill Clinton,
stood at the doors of Central High to welcome the Little
Rock Nine. Later that day President Bill Clinton presented
them with Congressional Gold Medals. The citation for the
medals included the commendation:

> *The Little Rock Nine risked their lives to integrate
> Central High School in Little Rock, Arkansas, and
> subsequently the nation.*
>
> *The Little Rock Nine sacrificed their innocence
> to protect the American principle that we are all one
> nation, under God, indivisible.*

How did the two students find their way to reconciliation and
friendship?

AN EXPERIENCE OF RACE IN AMERICA

Do you remember when you first became aware of race? I
was a young adult when Central High was desegregated. The
confrontation at the doors of Central High was disturbing
but it was not surprising. Racial conflict had been a fact of life
for as long as I could remember. I have tried to recall the
moment I discovered that some of us were black and others
were white. I had no such initial moment. Just as fish are
already in water and are unable to take notice of their habitat,
race was the context in which I was born and raised, and seg-

regation was the way things were. Life came in two basic varieties in my hometown—black and white. It seemed in the nature of things that these two groups lived in separate parts of town, went to separate schools and churches, had a different network of social contacts, and enjoyed well-defined boundaries of racial distancing. The main distinction marking their difference was that whites were assumed to be superior and that blacks were a lesser breed of humanity. The pattern was so clearly established that we hardly noticed unless the protocols were violated and the boundaries were breached.

If black toddlers wandered over to white water fountains or a black child rushed toward the white restroom or a black teenager sat at a lunch counter expecting to be served, their parents would quickly explain to them that blacks and whites did not use the same facilities. Black kids who sat down at the front of the bus had to be instructed about the seating arrangements, and if the weather was cold, they could take comfort from the fact that they were closer to the warmth of the motor in the back of the bus.

Sooner or later the inevitable questions were asked, I suspect, on both sides of town. Why? Why can't we play together? Why can't we go to the same schools? On the black side of town, kids asked, "Why do we have to sit in the balcony at the movie theater?" I wonder if the white kids asked their parents, "Why do they have to sit up there and we sit down here?" I am not sure what they were teaching in the white section of town, but the answers in my community were not usually satisfying. Instead, they were rather stoic resignations to the way things were, and our parents probably urged compliance for the sake of safety and survival. Sometimes there were muted protests: "They think they are better than we are." And other times resentment boiled over into acts of violence against the oppressive "etiquette" of race relations. Generally speaking, my community devised strategies for both endurance and for sustaining the dream that one day justice would prevail and the equal worth of all citizens would be affirmed.

By the time I reached adolescence I was highly sensitive to racist behavior and thinking. For example, our local radio station carried an editorial every morning. The commentator was Jesse Helms, who later became a senator from North Carolina. I remember distinctly that there were never any comments which affirmed my family, my church, or me. Always he seemed to speak against my people, against poor Negroes, against the oppressed. "My God!" I asked, "What is it with people who use their race as a dividing wall or a security blanket?" Pray for them, Jesus says. Pray for those who think security comes from their own race, their lifestyle, their political party, their sexual orientation, their wealth, their theology, or their nation. Pray for those who wrap themselves in a blanket of their own particular identities and block out the warmth and light of God's grace. In them, the Spirit dies, the soul is impoverished, and love is increasingly confined and smothered in a blanket of fear. What is it that makes them so insecure that they cannot even trust God, whom they claim to worship?

During my years of training for ministry, I began to see what was at work in the hearts and minds of those who were locked into prejudice and bigotry. I searched for a better understanding of what racism does to whites as well as blacks. I was desperate to discover if there was anything in my faith tradition strong enough to deliver our people from the grip of the demon-possession of racism. I spent many years searching for what would deliver us all from this congenital defect in our national psyche.

WHOSE GOSPEL TELLS THE TRUTH ABOUT RACIAL JUSTICE?

At the end of my second year as a student at Union Theological Seminary in New York City, I decided to take a year off to do an internship with my father, Bishop James A. Forbes Sr. He was serving as pastor of Providence Holy Church in Raleigh, North Carolina, my hometown. I interrupted my ministerial training to get some sense of what it would be like to serve as a minister in a Southern Pentecostal congregation after being trained at the predominately white, liberal Union Seminary. What I learned during that year reassured me that, although I was leaning toward a more progressive approach to the ministry, I could make a valuable contribution to the church of my youth. I felt a profound sense of gratitude for the role it had played in helping to shape my character and religious sensibilities. Some years later, one of my role models, Carlyle Marney, a white Southern Baptist minister, confirmed the wisdom of my choice. He said, "Jim, no man ever amounts to much until he learns to bless his own origins."

During that intern year on January 11, 1961, I had an experience I wrestled with throughout the next forty-seven years of my life. That day was the first time I was able to sit down and order a meal at the lunch counter of the Woolworth Five and Dime department store on Fayetteville Street in Raleigh.

I was twenty-five years old and I had lived my entire youth in the segregated South. I was thoroughly familiar with the etiquette and protocols of the Jim Crow Society: separation of black and white was the norm. I had experienced colored water fountains, colored restrooms, colored neighborhoods, colored schools, and colored churches, even colored hospitals and cemeteries. I knew the place assigned to me and my brothers and sisters of African descent.

In 1957, the year before I matriculated at Union Seminary, I had been reminded of that invisible but palpable line. I had applied to Duke Divinity School in Durham, North Carolina. Their letter of rejection explained that they did not accept Negro students, nor did they expect to do so in the foreseeable future. Many years later, when I spoke on Founder's Day at Duke University Chapel, I reminded the community of the letter I had received. My sermon that day was titled "Let's Forgive Our Fathers."

Things had begun to change only a few years after that Duke rejection. In 1960, beginning with sit-ins at a lunch counter in Greensboro, North Carolina, students from A&T University sparked a brushfire of civil disobedience protests. My brother David was then the student body president at Shaw University in Raleigh. He organized and led demonstrations at the local Woolworth store. After a brief struggle, the segregationist policy was dropped. At last, blacks could sit down for a meal at the counter rather than having to buy take-out lunches at a window. What a liberating moment! It symbolized the breaking of the chains of second-class citizenship. It was an answer to generations of mothers' and fathers' prayers that their sons and daughters would be respected as full human beings with all the rights and privileges of citizenship. It was Montgomery, Birmingham, and Selma—right there in my hometown. The battle for equality and justice had been fought and won. The Jericho walls were falling down everywhere, or so it seemed.

I felt a primal sense of delight as I made my way to the Woolworth store and sat down at the counter, ready to order lunch. Immediately after I sat down, the white woman sitting in the seat to my right got up and stormed out of the store! It was as if an illegal alien from another planet had invaded her sacred space. Her reaction shocked me to the core. It was such a disturbing moment that I cannot recall whether or not I eventually ordered the hot dog with catsup, mustard, and relish, and a big orange soda that I had anticipated consuming at that lunch counter.

My response was not simply a matter of how disturbed I was by her reaction. It was obvious that I had disturbed her deeply as well. I had been taught by my parents, church, and community not to do to others what I would not have done to me. I wondered what exposed nerve I had struck simply by making use of public services licensed to serve everybody and thereby claiming the right to be a full citizen. I wondered if she felt that I was a slightly less-human person than herself, or maybe she was afraid I intended some harm to her. Or maybe her distress was greater, as if her entire world was shaken. Perhaps my presence so close to her signaled that her protective wall of whiteness had sprung a leak that would flood her safe sanctuary of exclusion.

I can't remember if I ordered a meal that day, but I remember that I went home embarrassed, humiliated, hurt, and angry. I sat down and expressed my rage in a poem that I called "Thoughts at a Desegregated Lunch Counter":

Why did she move when I sat down?
Surely she could not tell so soon
That my Saturday bath had worn away
Or that savage passion
Had pushed me for a rape.

Perhaps it was the cash she carried in her purse;
She could not risk a theft so early in the month.
And who knew that on tomorrow t'would fall her lot
To drink her coffee from a cup
My darkened hands had clutched?

So horrible was that moment
I too should have run away
For prejudice has the odor of a dying beast.
Whether rapist or racist, both fall in the savage class
And the greatest theft of all is to rob one's right to be.

Long after I had forgotten the poem, it was returned to me thirty years later when I was the Senior Minister of The Riverside Church in New York City, a congregation that was 60 percent white and 40 percent black. A white parishioner had requested an appointment to meet with me. After we greeted each other, she explained the purpose of her visit: "I was going through some of my old letters when I ran across a letter that you sent me in 1961. It had this poem in it and I thought you might like to have it." It was the poem I had written after the Woolworth experience. I was startled both because she had kept it and because I wondered why I would send such an expression of pain and disappointment to a white woman living in the same Southern city as the woman who occasioned such anguish in my youthful, tender heart. Two white women, living in the same city. What was the difference?

I never again saw the woman who ran from the Woolworth lunch counter. I wish I could talk to her, to understand how she had experienced the event. I was sure that it was my black presence which had repelled her. Was it threat or disgust she felt? What was it that made it impossible for her to finish her meal while I was sitting at the counter next to her? A conversation with her might have given me insight into the deep chasm between some members of the white and black communities. I still regret that I never met her again or knew her name.

What I had sensed about my white parishioner when I knew her back in 1961 explains why I sent her a copy of my poem. Her name was Dorothy Marcus. At the time of the Woolworth incident she was a student at Meredith College in Raleigh, North Carolina, and working at the United Church on Hillsborough Street. The white congregation provided educational and recreational programs for young people in the black community. The spirit of her leadership and the genuineness of her counsel and care left me certain that what touched me deeply also mattered to her. I was sure that she would want to know what had happened to me and what could be done about it. I wanted to let her know about my fears and about my anger. Her caring witness reassured me that not all people are the same, even though they are of the same racial group.

By the time Dorothy Marcus returned my poem to me three decades later, she had moved north and was an active member of The Riverside Church. She was still involved in racial-justice work, seeking to move the church and society beyond racial polarization. She championed mutual respect, multicultural affirmation, and shared aspirations. Riverside was still struggling to understand racism, its roots, the various forms of its current manifestations, and its consequences. The Social Justice Commission of the church sponsored forums and workshops to explore ways to overcome the pernicious effects of racism and to safeguard coming generations against its viral toxicity. These church actions were a far cry from what I experienced thirty years before.

In the fall of 1961, after my intern year in Raleigh, I returned to Union Seminary. Freshly alerted to continuing racism, I signed up for a course on race taught by George Kelsey, a visiting professor from Drew University School of Theology. The principle resource for the course was his manuscript, later published as *Racism and the Christian Understanding of Man*. This course helped me probe more deeply the theological issues beneath racial prejudice, discrimination, and segregation. Kelsey explained that, for some people, race actually functions as a faith perspective. Racial oppression can be very strong and intractable because it operates on the level of religious commitment. The white woman who ran out of the Woolworth store was probably not aware of it, but she may have had a religiously held conviction about race! Dorothy Marcus, on the other hand, was bearing witness to the principles of her faith tradition as well when she reached out with love and understanding to Blacks. Conversations about racism and the power to overcome it are more fruitful if we are aware that we are dealing with two different and opposing "gospels." There is the "gospel of racial exceptionalism" and the "gospel of human equality of being."

My description of the two contrasting "gospels" and the attitudes and behaviors of those who hold them are sharply drawn here. While they may seem more extreme than what is found in individual members of either group, the clear distinctions show how deeply held convictions affect the way we think and feel about racial difference. While only the most extreme white supremacists might be accurately described by this entire description of the gospel of racism, many who would deny being racists might find themselves blushing at some of the ideas as being too close for comfort.

THE GOSPEL OF RACIAL EXCEPTIONALISM

The war in Iraq, saber rattling around the world, economic exploitation, political policies, and social deprivation—all of these bear strange resemblances to the gospel of racial exceptionalism. Racial exceptionalism finds parallel expressions in national exceptionalism. The same narrow, exclusionary spirit justifies invasions and occupations of other countries. Once the ideology of exceptionalism takes root in our hearts, it spreads like cancer into the cracks and crevices of our consciousness. It becomes highly resistant to efforts to overcome its all-consuming demand for loyalty. It is like a contagious addiction or like demon possession, even for those who want to be set free from its destructive power.

According to the doctrine of race as a religion, the racial characteristics of the in-group are the attributes of God. The white racist's God is white and confers sovereign power on whites. The other races are not divine like the special, elect white race, and whites, therefore, have a natural responsibility to define excellence and to preserve racial purity and their prerogatives of power. Thus, to be white and fail to be in charge of other races would make the white person a disappointment to God. The logic of this religion is circular: the ability to maintain superior power over other racial groups is compelling evidence of a special identification with God, since divinity confers special power to rule over others. At the same time, however, whites have the burden of maintaining the hierarchical differences, lest the foundational principles of white supremacy be undermined or exposed as illusory.

Just as God shows mercy to those who lack the glory and majesty of God, the white representatives of God should be in the position to show paternalistic care and kindness to the races beneath them. The faithful have to work to preserve the class differential and the hierarchy of the comparative worth of persons. Significant advancement in the ranks of the lesser races upsets the power system of paternalism. Whites must employ various methods to reduce the destabilizing dynamics of extraordinary excellence among other races and less than commendable behavior among whites. Strategies of segregation, discrimination, racial denigration, and violent punishment for challenging racism are designed to preserve what has already been mandated by God—according to race-based faith.

The gospel of such a faith preaches that the power of God belongs to the most God-like people. The superior group can feel assured and satisfied about themselves because there is always somebody else less valuable than themselves. Racism automatically confers many benefits upon whites. Pride, preferential treatment, and the freedom to pursue personal prerogatives come with the structures of white supremacy.

In addition to having material benefits like higher-paying jobs, elite education, exclusive housing, better medical attention, greater recreational opportunities, and special protection under the law, whites benefit from a moral double standard. The adjective "white" confers an illusion of superior ethical status and nobleness on whatever it modifies. Race-based faith suspends ethical sensibilities while pretending to be especially moral. Lynching, destructive medical experiments, denial of basic necessities, disproportional incarcerations, cultural denigration—all of these horrors and injustices should set off moral alarms in ethical human beings. But if race-based faith explains that whatever protects the interests of white supremacy is moral or at least exempt from moral judgment, moral alarm about barbaric brutalities and vast injustices would be unwarranted. One need not be outraged by the disparities between blacks and whites in infant mortality, life expectancy, unemployment, educational opportunity or cultural stigmatization, health care access, and inequities in the criminal justice system.

Whiteness justifies what whites do, even as the same behavior among blacks is condemned. Even the way we speak about lies reflects this double standard: a white lie is less evil than a plain lie. If white people stick together and protect their principles and racial purity, they reinforce their right to rule the world and regulate the affairs of everyone else on God's behalf.

Race-based faith requires the creation of subspecies; people of different races are viewed as a lesser breed within the species. The audacity of subordinating other people usurps the authority of God, who is the creator of us all as manifestations of the divine image. Those who tamper with the handiwork of God have replaced true divinity with an egocentric deity of human construction. The concept of race itself is an artificial construct that creates a false hierarchy among human beings. Whenever any human entity is made the measure of all things, inevitable disasters in ethical judgment occur. Race-based faith justified whites enslaving other people. The decision to take Africans from their land to be sold as chattel property in the Americas was based on the doctrine that they were dark savages and not really human beings. In fact, white paternalism viewed them as being rescued from their subhuman condition. In permanent servitude in a civilized land, they could be enlightened with only the minor drawback of oppressive and dehumanizing conditions. Such notions of white superiority made possible the genocide of Native Americans before and during the mass importation of African slaves. Race-based faith frequently recruits persons of color, who accept racial hierarchy and perform well in its dehumanizing system, as leaders to discipline their own.

This theoretical profile of race posing as religion sets forth the theological seeds which sprout and grow into violent and destructive action. Once established, racist practices are extremely difficult to bring to an end. Holocausts and genocides, crusades and apartheids begin as ideas that later become intractable systems of oppression. The practices of racial and tribalistic prejudice become poison to a whole system. They affect language, patterns of social interaction, political and economic policies, and everyday patterns of life. With the spirit of racism firmly in place, relegating minorities to second-class status and creating glaring inequities does not seem to require either explanation or remediation. It's just the way things are, as God designed it.

When race is a religion, it absolutely defines meaning, identity, and official protection. Race-based faith is guilty, however, of fraudulent advertising because reality defies doctrines of racial superiority. Science suggests that the differences between the races are less than racism asserts, and anyone paying attention to moral behavior will find whites no more or less exemplary than anyone else. Virtue and vice, strength and weakness, intelligence and stupidity are evenly distributed among all races. Maya Angelou says in her poem "Human Family":

> I note the obvious differences
> between sort and type,
> but we are more alike, my friends
> than we are unalike.[2]

When people bow at the altar of racial superiority, they set themselves on a course that leads to false hopes, fictitious claims, faulty self-assessment and flawed relationships among members of different races. Distorted thinking and fear robs them of the genuine presence of those who are different. It produces suspicious and unnecessary mistrust. Vigilante corps of boundary patrols keep out the truth of our mutual dependence and the benefits of multicultural exchange. When people rely on surface appearances and false racial stereotypes, rather than in-depth knowledge of others at the level of the heart, mind, and spirit, their ability to assess and understand people accurately is compromised. The god-of-race makes us run away from people and feel safer in the confines of sameness. Our fear produces knee-jerk spasms of avoidance and isolation. What a colossal waste of precious energy to create such a sad, sorry loneliness!

THE GOSPEL OF HUMAN RACE
EQUALITY OF BEING

The gospel of human race equality is grounded in the justice and love of the ultimate source of being, the Creator of us all. The God who made us loves each of us as parents, who love all their children. God loves us with complete commitment to our well-being. Our worth is the gracious gift of divine love. The attempt of human beings to claim ultimacy is the height of usurpation, rebellion, and apostasy. We are finite. God, who is infinite, loves us all the same. Our fundamental worth as persons is solely determined by that declaration of love and nothing else.

Martin Luther King Jr.'s vision of the "world house" describes our ties of family based on this love. According to Dr. King, we are like members of a family who have been tragically separated from each other. Upon the death of our parents, we inherited the house under the condition that we must learn to live together in the house in harmony. The various races have inherited the world as a house and can survive in it only if we see each other as one vast family. As the loving parent of the household of humankind, God agonizes over our bigotry, arrogance, and self-vaulting pride. In order to restore the sense of fundamental worth to anyone deprived of it, God takes up the task of building our original equality of worth. God is the prime advocate for the dispossessed, despised, or rejected members of the human family in order to restore the whole house to its integrity of equality.

Such equality does not mean that everyone is of equal intelligence or equal healthfulness. We are not equal in character, equal in compassion, or equal in aptitude for various kinds of work. But these differences are secondary considerations when we see everyone as a child of God. The gospel of human race equality of being encourages us to view people through the eyes of God. This is good news when we pause to consider the words of the psalmist, "If you, O Lord should mark iniquities, Lord who could stand?" (Psalm 130:3). Or, as I've often remarked, no one is going to pass God's course on righteousness unless God is grading on a curve. Indeed, self-righteousness is one trait which causes any one of us to earn a failing grade when God is doing the evaluation. God's offer of loving regard in equal measure to all is a positive arrangement. The Spirit seeks to recruit us into the Beloved Community, where our standing as equals is conferred by grace alone.

When we face the choice of either the gospel of exceptionalism and race-based faith or the gospel of human race equality, our decision is a spiritual decision of ultimate significance. How we live our lives rests upon our response to either the call of the Spirit or the call of the self-idolatry impulse at the heart of racist thinking. If we respond positively to God's gracious urging, we will turn the gated enclave of racism into the true community of human equality.

THE POWER TO ANSWER THE CALL

Despite the Spirit's call to us to become a nonracial society, we have not yet thrown off the shackles of racist thinking. In 1993, William Sloane Coffin, former Senior Minister of The Riverside Church, gave this assessment in his book *A Passion for the Possible:*

> For whatever reason—be it the blindness of sightless souls, the indifference of distracted people, or just plain compassion fatigue—whatever the reasons, the majority of white Americans do not feel the monstrosity of inequality so universally felt today by

black Americans. The result is that racism remains bone-deep in American society.[3]

The disgraceful revelations following Hurricane Katrina made the truth of Coffin's words highly visible. The plight of the poor and black people of New Orleans was laid bare for all to see. The impoverished living conditions existing before the flood became an indictment against the city of New Orleans but, in a real sense, it became an exposé about inner-city life all across our nation. Compassionate responses to the Katrina crisis have been impressive, coming from houses of worship, corporations, community agencies, and concerned individuals. However, charity is not enough; in-depth structural changes to promote justice are urgently needed.

I had hoped that Katrina would become a teachable moment about race and class in America and that serious efforts would be made to address the problems of the underbelly of our society. More than the repair of levees was needed. Rebuilding of the infrastructure of the community was crucial, to be sure, but there were fundamental questions to be raised and policy issues to be resolved.

Katrina exposed the glaring inequities between the basic subsistence of the black and white poor of the community. Long indifference to these disparities and the cost to communities of these inequalities belied our vision of democracy with the truth of two Americas. Thus far, it appears our nation is unwilling to invest in the elimination of the disparities between blacks and whites. After a brief period of attention to inequality following Katrina's devastation, the issue of race was once again tucked away so that we could concentrate on the Iraq war and ominous signs on the horizon about the economy.

But the issue of race did not go away. It forced itself back into the open during the campaign for president of the United States in 2008. For the first time in our history, a black man won the bid to be the Democratic Party candidate. Despite efforts to show that race did not matter, it kept announcing itself as a factor in the election. At first the discussion was subtle and uncomfortable, but before long it was out in the open. Barack Obama gave what was widely regarded as a brilliant speech on race after the controversy his opponents stirred up over his former pastor, Dr. Jeremiah Wright. The press reported on polling data suggesting certain population groups would not vote for a black man. Perhaps the most challenging tightrope Obama walked was how to be himself as a person of mixed-race parentage, given the racial attitude across the country. The campaign made it abundantly clear that race and racism still matter, powerfully.

Meanwhile the Spirit is still seeking to recruit us to be a part of the beloved community of racial justice and equality. Some persons and families have answered the call. One of the most powerful accounts of a family deciding to deal with race is told in a film documentary called *Traces of the Trade*, narrated and produced by Katrina Browne.[4] The story begins when Katrina is reading family history accounts written by her grandmother. In it is a reference that the family had been involved in the slave trade. That detail sparked a burning desire to know more about that aspect of her family's history. Her desire led her to Bristol, Rhode Island, where her family, the DeWolfs, were the revered leaders of the community and prominent in business and religion. Under their leadership the entire town developed various aspects of the slave trade that brought significant financial benefits. The local Episcopal church counted the DeWolfs among their principal benefactors and congregants. They had paid for the stained-glass windows. A very lucrative slave-trading enterprise, based on a triangle between Ghana, Rhode Island, and Cuba, fueled their largess. They picked up sugar and molasses in Cuba; refined it into rum in Bristol, Rhode Island; and took rum to Ghana in exchange for slaves to be brought back to the Caribbean and Charleston, South Carolina. This business was so profitable that James DeWolf became the second richest man in the United States.

At least three generations of DeWolfs were involved in some aspect of the slave trade, such as banking, shipbuilding, distillery equipment manufacturing, or the making of chains and leg irons to secure the slaves. Even the insurance business became important for the high-risk/high-return trading operation. Much of this lucrative business took place long after the slave trade had become illegal.

The family and town tacitly agreed not to talk about the shameful chapter in the DeWolfs' past. The rule was, "Don't sully the name." But Katrina Browne felt that the issue had to be faced. Their mental, emotional, and spiritual health required it. So she decided to invite as many of the extended family as were willing to join her in a journey to retrace the routes that had been taken by their ancestors in their slave trafficking. Out of the nearly two hundred people who were invited, ten were willing to take the journey with her. They began in Bristol, reviewing long-ignored documents chronicling various details of the family's involvement. They then went to the slave-holding compounds on Cape Coast, Ghana. After reliving the rituals and transactions of the exchange of goods for slaves, they returned to Cuba where sugarcane was grown on plantations formerly worked by slaves. Finally they returned to Bristol to debrief the experience and decide what they needed to do to redeem the family name.

Each member who participated made a personal decision about what their moral integrity and family pride demanded of them. Some accepted the duty of communicating their findings with members of the family who did not go on the journey. Some made special outreach efforts to other whites. Still others worked with people of color in hopes of promoting truth and reconciliation commissions. Some family members felt reparations were an important step toward acknowledging that beneficiaries of the slave trade ought to participate in concrete efforts to rebuild what had been torn down. They thought that businesses should be contacted to determine if those who had benefited from the institution of slavery would be willing to take responsibility for projects of restoration.

The experience of searing truth released the members of the DeWolf family from denial, guilt, and shame. They will never again be able to view their privilege without the awareness that it came at the price of the material and psychic impoverishment of millions of people of color. Their faith in equality holds them to account for helping our nation to answer the call to be the beloved community.

Let us return to Little Rock and our story of Hazel Bryan, who through marriage became Hazel Bryan Massy and was the white student in the Little Rock photo described at the beginning of the chapter. As her three children were growing up, she changed her racial attitudes. She knew her racist actions at Central High were not right and started contemplating what atonement she might make. Remembering the photograph of her taunting Elizabeth Eckford, Hazel continued to feel like she was "the poster child for the hate generation, trapped in the image captured in the photograph, and I knew that my life was more than that moment." Hazel called Elizabeth to apologize in 1963. But it was in 1997 that they had the opportunity to meet face to face. Will Counts, who captured the tension of that day in 1957 with his camera, was the one to make arrangements for Hazel and Elizabeth to meet during the Fortieth Anniversary Commemoration of the desegregation of Central High. After breaking the awkward ice together, they embraced and began a life-long friendship. They continued to work together to build racial harmony in their communities.

The photograph had made it possible for Hazel to see herself back then, and she didn't like what she saw. She refused to be defined by the passion of that moment. Why should she be trapped in a time warp of hatred? She saw herself and resolved to do something about it. She was ready to accept the invitation to become a part of the Beloved Community not defined by race.

What is needed to move us beyond racism and its psychic infrastructure of prejudice and hate is an experience which lets us truly see ourselves. Perhaps just a flash as quick as the shutter's eye will be enough. An in-depth glance at the shadow within may be enough to set us in a new direction.

It may be too late to arrange a photograph of reconciliation between the white woman at the Woolworth lunch counter and me from fifty years ago. Recently I shared the story about the lunch counter experience during an interview with Bill Moyers on PBS. I wondered if she was watching that night. Perhaps so! Or maybe not. At least I can keep on writing and preaching in the hope of providing a mirror that will help us see ourselves, as I also seek to be mindful of my own blind spots. That may be one of the ways the Spirit works to cast out other "isms" of exclusion—knowing we all have blind spots.

Martin Luther King Jr. wrote his first book, *Stride Toward Freedom*, to describe the Montgomery Bus Boycott. In it he said, "The Holy Spirit is the continuing community-creating reality which moves through history." In the book of the Acts of the Apostles, Chapter 10, an account of Simon Peter shows how he was able to see himself and, in the light of what he saw, become willing to follow the Spirit in a community-building mission.

In the Acts story, the time had come to break down the barrier between Jewish Christians and the Gentile community. The Spirit had chosen Peter to speak for the mission to the Gentiles, which was something he had not done before. Peter very strictly adhered to the customs and traditional prohibitions of his Jewish people. In order to release Peter to the new calling, he had to have a change of perception on a very deep level. The Spirit arranged a life-transforming experience that enabled Peter to see himself and others in a completely new light. While waiting for something to eat, he fell into a trance:

He saw the heaven opened and something like a large sheet coming down, being lowered to the ground by its four corners. In it were all kinds of four-footed creatures and reptiles and birds of the air. Then he heard a voice saying, "Get up, Peter, kill and eat." But Peter said, "By no means, Lord; for I have never eaten anything that is profane or unclean." The voice said to him again, a second time, "What God has made clean, you must not call profane." This happened three times, and the thing was suddenly taken up to heaven. (Acts 10:11–16)

Through this trance, Peter was able to see himself as so locked into his tradition that he would let it trump a mandate from God. The powers of the picture he received through the trance made him ready to undertake the mission and open up a new phase in the development of his faith. The trance ends with a reference to the transformative experience Peter had undergone. The text says, "and the thing was suddenly taken up to heaven."

What a powerful image—"the thing." The thing helps us see who we really are. The thing then shows us the will of God in the particular situation, and the thing helps us see other people in a completely new light.

We stand between two gospels about race—the gospel of racial exceptionalism and the gospel of human race equality of being. To help us make the just and righteous choice, we may need a "thing from heaven." It may be the best hope for becoming a nonracial society. As we are alert and keep our spirits open to the truth that comes to us in many different ways, perhaps we will see a picture of ourselves, our community, and our world that we know does not honor our Creator. The Spirit provides the picture and also offers us forgiveness and power to become fully alive members of the Beloved Community.

4

Economic Justice:
Are All the Children In?

As a child in the 1940s, I lived at 915 South Bloodworth Street in Raleigh, North Carolina. The house was a three-bedroom parsonage. There were ten folks in that house. Mama and Daddy slept in one bedroom, the girls in another, and the boys in still another, with multiple shared beds to accommodate everyone. Daddy worked in a W.T. Grant's Department Store, and Mama rose early in the morning to ride the bus across town to work as a domestic in white homes. My parents had eight children to support, and they worked very hard to provide for such a large family.

One day, at my elementary school, a big truck pulled up with bags of cabbage for children from poor families. I went to the back of the truck to wait for my cabbage. I thought it would be a blessing for the family. When they opened the door, I smelled the cabbages. They were rotting. Still, I picked up a sack and took one across town to my home. Mama, always gracious, said, "Thank God, son, all we have to do is go out to the back porch and peel off the rotten part and take the rest of it. We will make something." We had cabbage that afternoon. I learned that you may receive a sack of rotten food, but take what you can and make what you can of it.

The cabbage from the back of that truck led to many questions for me. If they want to give out cabbages, can't they at least be fresh? If they want to spread around a little bit of charity, why can't it be out of the best they have, instead of spoiled goods? At school, it became obvious to me that, when we picked up our books in the beginning of the year, they always had writing inside because the books were first read across town at the white school. We got their leftover, used books. It was a long time before I saw a brand new book. By the time I reached high school, I found myself increasingly outraged by the gap between the haves and the have nots.

As we grow up, as we increase our resources, get a little education, enjoy a little class mobility, it is possible to forget the sensitivity nurtured in us years ago. And it is even possible to walk past the poor and harden ourselves against their cries. "A little money, please? I am hungry, can you give me a dime? Mister, won't you help me?" One day while walking down the street eating an ice cream cone, a homeless woman approached me and said, "I would like Häagen Dazs ice cream too. Can't you give me a cone?" Over the years, we sometimes adjust to the wide gap between the haves and the have nots and forget that poor people like nice things.

The God Christians worship says that they are all my children. They all matter. God cares for them. God wants them to have all that is necessary for life. Our God, I believe, says you can have your nice things as far as I'm concerned. But my children must have the basic resources for existence, for without that, they cannot aspire to the fullness I intended for them.

While our nation debates whether health care is a right or just a potential benefit, if you're lucky, the fundamental tenets of our faith shout out to us: "In God's eyes, it is a right for all." If persons have been blessed with surplus income or staggering salaries and bonuses and consider themselves to be Christians, why would they be resistant to universal health care? If a nation has been rescued from economic collapse, wouldn't it seem that gratitude to God would take the form of a desire to work toward a more just society? If we are really sincere when we pray God Bless America, it would seem natural for us to bless the Lord by caring for the most vulnerable among us. President Ronald Reagan used to appeal for support by saying, "Do it for the Gipper." In regards to health care and economic justice, I wish people of faith would join me in saying to our nation, "Do it for God."

Jesus asks us if it matters to us that some of us have enough bread or more than enough to spare, and others perish from hunger? Does it matter that some of us have health care benefits and others are without access to the most basic medical care? Do we really care that some of us have housing while others have no place they can call home? Beyond these most basic needs, Jesus asks if we notice those who are without gainful and meaningful employment—the long term unemployed and the most recently laid off. Does it matter to us, to God? How do we condone the consumption of 40 percent of the world's resources by 5 percent of the world's population? How does such economic disparity impact the heart of God? How does our God regard these things?

Matthew 25:31–40 has one answer:

> When the Son of Man comes in his glory, and all the
> angels with him, then he will sit on the throne of his
> glory. All the nations will be gathered before him,
> and he will separate them one from another as a
> shepherd separates the sheep from the goats, and he
> will put the sheep at his right hand, but the goats at
> the left. Then the King will say to those at his right
> hand, "Come, you that are blessed by my Father,
> inherit the kingdom prepared for you from the foun-
> dation of the world; for I was hungry and you gave
> me food, I was thirsty and you gave me something to
> drink, I was a stranger and you welcomed me, I was
> naked and you gave me clothing, I was sick and you
> took care of me, I was in prison and you visited me."
> Then the righteous will answer him, "Lord, when
> was it that we saw you hungry and gave you food, or
> thirsty and gave you something to drink? And when
> was it that we saw you a stranger and welcomed you,
> or naked and gave you clothing? And when was it
> that we saw you sick or in prison and visited you?"
> And the king will answer them, "Truly I tell you, just
> as you did it to one of the least of these who are
> members of my family, you did it to me."

In this word from Jesus is a call from God to build a new
inclusive class, a class of people who will recognize that we
are all one family—these are the people Jesus came to heal
and liberate. We are all the offspring of the same heavenly

Mother and Father. We are all equally assured of the opportunity to develop our fullness until God can say, now that is what I had in mind, this human thriving in every dimension.

ARE ALL THE CHILDREN IN?

My childhood house had three bedrooms and many beds, but we had only one dining room table. We used every leaf in the table to seat us all. At dinner, Mama often began with a little ritual. When we were finally ready to say the grace she would ask, "Are all the children in?" We had to look around because, with a family of our size, plus the guests that often joined us, we might not notice if somebody was missing. If we observed that somebody was missing, we were to speak up. Then, we were permitted to say the grace, but we could not fill our plates with food until we first prepared a plate for the missing member. That extra plate of food went into the oven of the old wood-burning stove to keep it warm until the missing person arrived.

My mother raised us to know that the first act after grace—the first thing we must do as our expression of gratitude for the blessings of God—was to prepare a plate for those not yet at the table. Her ethic of love, of preparing a portion of the feast for others before we could enjoy it ourselves, became a part of my consciousness before I even thought about it, before I went to seminary, and before I was a minister.

In my South Bloodworth Street home, I learned the ritual and the values of gratitude and generosity that lie at the core of my understanding of the Christian gospel. God's good news is that the one dining room table is big enough for every human being because Jesus Christ is the host of the table, and He turns no one away from the feast.

The feast is, of course, far more than one good meal a day, though there are far too many in the world who do not get even one good meal a week. The feast is abundant life, promised by Jesus Christ and delivered through his spirit, the Holy Spirit. That Spirit must inspire Christians together to assure everyone that they are invited to the table where God has promised full servings of health, strength, dignity, education, freedom, and love that sustains a vibrant life. And God has kept the promise! Yet as so often happens, our avarice and greed have not led us to share the servings. We are not asking the critical question; "Are all the children in?"

The mortgage crisis of 2007 brought the shadow of homelessness beyond the poor to the world of the struggling middle class. We saw increasing evidence of worsening health conditions due to the lack of basic health care coverage. We were in a tough time, spending trillions on an immoral war while depriving wounded veterans and their families of health care and basic necessities. While the super rich built homes the size of luxury hotels for two or three people to live in, children became increasingly homeless. Something has gone terribly, terribly wrong in our society, in the richest nation in the world. The children are not all finding a place at the feasting table of the Lord.

Something has happened to us. We are not a happy society. Even those who have some resources are discovering that they are not adequate, and those who have plenty feel insecure and deprived. The breakdown of our common welfare is the result of a spiritual crisis in our times. The patterns of economic injustice became a matter of spiritual impoverishment when people forget there is a God who wants and expects better of us. Even if we like our nice things, if we bury our compassion for other children and families, we abandon what gives us life, the spiritual, moral core of our lives.

Norman Lear has said:

> I cannot explain how we have arrived at this point. It may be enough to note that a radical shift has occurred over the past 40 years in the institutions that guide and direct our culture. Once we looked to the church, the synagogue, the family, the community and civil authorities. But clearly that grand ancestral order has waned. Where we drift as a society is determined today more by the decisions of corporate managers and the values that dictate their decisions, than by any other single influence. Short-term thinking, corrosive individualism, fixating on economic demands—these are some of the forces that now pervade our culture at the expense of the human spirit, since business has become the fountainhead of values in the society.[1]

Lear suggests that the waning of family ties and religious institutions has left a vacuum, and mass entertainment has invaded our homes with the value of constant consumerism and corporate values. Lear quotes Stewart Ewin, author of *Captains of Consciousness, Channels of Desire,* and *All Consuming Images*, as having often written, "Market forces have become the new value system and we have come to the point where advertisers have become the primary mode of public address. The term consumer has become a substitute for the word citizen, and the word truth is simply that which sells."

Jesus said he came with the ministry of teaching, of preaching, and of healing. He gathered people and made disciples who understood the nature and the will of God. Jesus called his disciples and sat down and taught them to create a new community of people. God's will is fulfilled when there is good news for the poor. In this new community, the poor are blessed; they are the children for whom a warm plate of food waits. We are all called to enter the gates of the Beloved Community. The good news is we are a brand-new fellowship, a new community of people gathered around the table, where all the children are in.

The Realm of God is difficult for the rich to enter because their material well-being tempts them to be less sensitive to spiritual dimensions of life. They are able to order what they want without having to think of the impact of their use of money on the rest of the community. Their money enables them to shape the culture according to their influence and may lead to the exploitation of others. They will have trouble getting in, Jesus says, because in order to get in we all have to recognize that without God we would be nothing; without God we fail to be faithful to each other. There are some very important things we cannot buy, like friendship, good health, and soul satisfaction. I wonder if when some millionaires lie down to die that they first become aware of the limitation of their vast treasure. Alas, their money cannot save them. Jesus tells the story of the rich young ruler. He sensed a need for value beyond his wealth. He wanted what his culture called eternal life. Jesus told him to sell his possessions, give to the poor, and come follow me. In response, the young man said, "No deal" because of the stranglehold of his possessions (Matthew 19:16–22). Jesus knew, if you hold on to your material resources as your pearl of great price, you will forfeit the deeper meaning of life. You will stop short of the goal in the race. It will be like dropping out of college the last quarter before graduation. Don't let your need for your comfort and don't let the power of the things you possess rob you of being a person who reaches the goal of serving God and the Kingdom.

Jesus came to gather a new group of people, people who will be brothers and sisters together at the one table of God. Grateful for the blessings of God, this new group of people will understand that their security is in God. People ready to enter into the reign of God will work to build a society that eliminates its inequities and disparities. People of God will build a new order, not only where the basic necessities for existence are available to all people and where none of us will seek to hoard for ourselves, but also where all have what they need to thrive and reach their full potential.

From God's view, everyone deserves the opportunity for fulfilling his or her destiny, none more than anyone else. God asks, "Are all the children in?" and has made provisions for our well-being; a warm plate awaits us. If there are those who are poor, who are without food, clothing, shelter, without meaningful forms of work, without some opportunity for leisure, without some opportunity for the joyful side of life, if there is anybody who is without these, then, in a real sense, she or he is our responsibility. What Jesus has to say to us is that we who are willing to enter the Kingdom of God must learn how to be agents of love in a special way. We must give up our addiction to things that satisfy us, unless we are also able to help provide resources that meet the needs of others.

To close the unjust social and economic resource chasm, we must first of all create an economic bill of rights. We have a responsibility to elaborate and articulate, like never before, at least what the basic standards of human existence ought to be for anyone who is not just a consumer, but a citizen of the world God created, a standard below which we will never allow our fellow human beings to fall. Our government is beholden to corporate largesse and lobbyists, so that most politicians will find it politically risky to support an economic bill of rights. However, if they intend to follow their commitment to the oath of office, they must take the risk. We need a congress and a president of any party who is committed to an economic bill of rights.

Can you imagine these words being addressed to our nation by a president during a State of the Union address?

In our day these economic truths have become accepted as self-evident. We have accepted, so to speak, a second Bill of Rights under which a new basis of security and prosperity can be established for all—regardless of station, race, or creed. It was during President Franklin D. Roosevelt's January 11, 1944, message to Congress that this challenge was presented to the American people. He did not stop with a general admonition to economic justice but went on to outline his "Economic Bill of Rights."

Among these are:

The right to a useful and remunerative job in the industries or shops or farms or mines of the nation;

The right to earn enough to provide adequate food and clothing and recreation;

The right of every farmer to raise and sell his products at a return which will give him and his family a decent living;

The right of every businessman, large and small, to trade in an atmosphere of freedom from unfair competition and domination by monopolies at home or abroad;

The right of every family to a decent home;

The right to adequate medical care and the opportunity to achieve and enjoy good health;

The right to adequate protection from the economic fears of old age, sickness, accident, and unemployment;

The right to a good education.

America's own rightful place in the world depends in large part upon how fully these and similar rights have been carried into practice for our citizens.

We in the church enjoy making a list of what the government ought to do. It is equally important to make a list of what church members ought to be doing. Here is a starter list. We must tithe, an old biblical principle of devoting 10 percent of what we receive to the care of others. It is surprising how powerful a symbol it is to give an offering as an investment in God's new reign of justice and compassion. We might have to inch our way along to reach 10 percent, but the struggle must make us sisters and brothers who are strongly committed to rising above an addiction to our own things. Without breaking our addictions to our own stuff, we will not be able to meet the needs of the poor and the oppressed. It will take a mighty effort to transform the church and the society, but we have to begin with ourselves and uphold a tithing standard as the minimum we share with others. Only then will our congregations be empowered to care for the least among us and to fill the plates of the destitute first—and we will, if we can do this, find there is more than enough for all.

In my most ideal moments, I do not think we can consider ourselves mature and conscientious Christians until we are able to give a double tithe: a tithe to the church and a tithe to other causes. We must figure out a way to live on the other 80 percent. I, too, enjoy my nice things, but I am convinced that until we are serious enough to let our religion hit us in the pocketbook and until our money is offered up along with our hearts, we will not join the new community of people Jesus tried to develop. There are times and seasons when it is not possible to raise this level of stewardship but it is a standard to which we should aspire. The new network of people will have compassion and a spirit of sacrifice. Sacrifice and compassion are how, in an unjust, unequal society, we will work toward the realization of the realm of God. The sacrificial giving and compassionate care of the religious communities cannot be a substitute for services which should be funded from our tax dollars. The mere mention of taxes awakens conflict and generates heated debate. It is such a sensitive matter that it becomes a litmus-test in most political campaigns. Candidates are required to assure the electorate that "I will not raise your taxes," even though fulfilling campaign promises will surely demand revenue from somewhere. In short, it is unlikely that an in-depth analysis of the values reflected in our tax policy will come from officials who have to stand for election. Perhaps the faith community is the only place where such a review can take place. Given the mystery, machinations, loopholes, and reticence to engage in tax discussions, religious leaders have a responsibility to convene that conversation in which questions like the following are faced with utmost seriousness:

1. What are the fundamental principles underlying our tax policy?
2. What is the formula by which we measure the fairness of tax assessments?
3. What moral issues are reflected in the way governments levy taxes and budget the use of tax revenues?
4. What class biases are operating in the present policy and how may they be addressed?
5. How might our tax policy best embody the democratic ideals of our nation's founding spirit? (e.g., "that all are created equal and are endowed by our Creator with certain inalienable rights among which are life, liberty, and the pursuit of happiness")

We who are members of faith communities have an obligation to press for a more just tax policy. Even if our neighbors are fighting against raising taxes, we must ask what tax assessment will lead to the most fair distribution of resources in our cities and across the nation.

We need to develop a theology of "enough." In our Exodus story about God providing manna for the Israelites as they made their way to the promised land, they are instructed to gather only enough. If they gathered more than they needed it would spoil. Grasping for more and more, eating more than we need, hoarding vast reserves—these all suggest anxiety about enough. In addition to the problem of obesity from overeating, there is the super-sized sense of need. This can lead to a constant state of feeling that there is never enough. In fact, the anxiety about enough may be so pervasive that it has led to the epidemic of greed in our society.

In addition to adventurous phantom investments and irresponsible deregulation, greed was considered to be a major factor in global economic collapse in 2007–2008. As we look forward to the recovery of a sound and stable economy, we will need to address the American state of mind that there is not enough. We will need to experience trust enough in God, each other, and a just system of production and distribution to relax from obsessive acquisitiveness. A communal commitment to the development of a theology of enough draws us closer to the kind of world God wills us to be. While we prepare to restructure for such a world, we must remember that in the world as it is there are those who have nothing because we consume more than enough.

Church members and pastoral staff need to take better

care of each other and the larger community in times of special need. Illness, domestic violence, child abuse, job loss, and parenting are examples of the myriad experiences that may confront us in our life journey. Whoever joins a church ought to take a pledge and be given a pledge of support from the congregation to find ways to be helpful in a person's hours of distress. Along with being comforters and friends, churches must offer resources or skills such as parenting, coping with crises, marital enrichment, living with illness, and money management, along with other learning opportunities to relieve one another's burdens and enrich the abilities of all to live life in a spirit of peace and justice. We should show through our own practices that we affirm a relationship between spiritual needs and temporal material well-being. The spirit of the congregation should be one of mutual care and shared responsibility. And our public citizenship energy ought to go to making sure that municipal, state, and federal policies place human needs at the core of their commitments. And then, as we meet our needs, we ought to move steadily to increase the portion of our budget that we give to the outside. Churches that have committed to giving away 50 percent of their money become a model, some do exist and others are inching their way to half.

Equity must become the norm. We must look for ways to narrow the economic gap every chance we get. While everybody else is backing up and the gap keeps widening, the Christian church along with other faith traditions must come forward and impact this nation's consciousness and conscience. We must insist on greater accountability for the tax dollars we pay, until there is greater accountability to a humanizing agenda. In actuality, we have a responsibility as taxpayers to contribute to national security, sound infrastructure, maintenance of justice, and other essentials for the public good. While we cultivate the spirit of enough, we must also demand that a fair portion of our tax dollars feed the hungry, clothe the naked, house those who have no home, and heal the sick.

THE BLESSINGS OF GENEROSITY

When God asks us to give, we are not so much asked to make a contribution as we are asked to make a commitment. We present our bodies as a living sacrifice, wholly acceptable unto God. We may keep our jobs, keep our homes, keep some of our assets, but we are giving ourselves. When we give ourselves, what we keep for ourselves will be used according to kingdom values and what we give to the church will also be used in relationship to the kind of world God intends. By such giving, we sustain a living and loving relationship to God. Our possessions become instruments by which we express our gratitude and our love to God. We begin to be a part of a time, a time that moves toward the realm of God, part of a people, a people who will collectively transform their communities to make food available for the hungry, clothing for those who are naked, shelter for those who are without, and health care for all.

When we give ourselves to building the realm of God, we come to understand the ultimate meaning of life. While we all look forward to better days, we must also be prepared for dark and cloudy days. We become less afraid that a reduction in our income is going to spell the end of us. It is possible in those circumstances that we will have more joy, we will have more hope, we will have more confidence, and we will have more peace. Jesus was definitely on to something. We can become agents of God, by which God can use us and our resources to meet the world's needs. We can become a company of those who want to fulfill the divine dream of justice and peace, and we can feel the power of conscientious investment in the world that God wants us to create. The more we give out of a heart of gratitude, the more God enriches the quality of our lives. When God asks us, "Are all the children in?" we will be able to say, "Yes, we are all here."

5

In War:
Which Commandments Are Broken?

In the beginning, many religious leaders called the Iraq War immoral, illegal, and unwise. How easy it is to forget how much against the tide it was to oppose the war when it started in March 2003. Such witness required great courage at the time. Religious leaders said prayers for peace. Many people of faith supported soldiers of conscience who refused to serve, led memorials for the fallen, held peace marches and peace services—some of us even got arrested. As was the case in other wars before, ministers preached and preached against the war and even spoke to our congressional representatives. Yet, even as the scandals of torture and evidence of war profiteering grew, the killing continued. The American people increasingly wanted an end while the Iraqi people could hardly be awakened from their nightmare of war to rebuild their homes and lives. To pay for the war, funds from the health and welfare of our own citizens were exhausted; abandoned wounded veterans were subjected to substandard or little care; and the national debt swelled to multi-trillions. The relentless slaughter went unabated. Our war efforts exposed us to less than the high ground of democratic values. What are the moral failures that were manifested in the United States initiation and continuation in this war?

Those moral failures are especially agonizing when you consider how many of the strongest proponents for the war, then and now, are Christians, and not just Christians, but Bible-believing Christians. Calling war illegal, immoral, or unjust comes from just-war theory. It comes to us from St. Augustine of Hippo who drew much of what he said from earlier Greek and Roman traditions. For Bible-believing Christians, and I count myself as one of them, what the Bible says is crucial. But what does the Bible say about war and moral failures?

THE TEN COMMANDMENTS OF PEACE

A good place to look for guidance is the Ten Commandments in Exodus 20. Both Jews and Christians understand that God speaks to us in a list of standards and that these commandments shape the ethical dimensions of our faith. I wonder, however, how many Christians who recite them have actually thought about what they might mean. Jesus captured them in one sentence when he said we should love God with all our heart, mind, soul, and strength, and our neighbors as ourselves.

At least one Christian, a judge in Alabama, was willing to violate the constitutional separation of church and state by posting the commandments inside his court room. Later, he was forced to remove them. While I support that principle of separation and do not want our government used to enforce one faith on everyone, I also suspect that, if more of our government leaders actually had to follow the commandments, we would have a very different country and a different world.

Conservatives and progressives can exchange views about them, but we must not forget that the Ten Commandments come from the prophetic traditions of the Bible. Moses is counted as the first prophet because he led the Israelites out of slavery and then delivered these commandments from God about how the community should live. My interpretation of them springs from that prophetic branch of the Christian faith.

War violates all Ten Commandments. There is no getting around it. How it does so is a matter of interpretation, but any honest reading of the list makes it hard to deny that God forbids war. Of course the Bible contains instances in which a particular war seems to be encouraged, but the bedrock principle of biblical obedience to divine will makes war evil, even though in some instances it appears to be a necessary evil. Even then, it should only be chosen after every other alternative has failed. A militaristic spirit runs afoul of God's call to justice and peace. Hence, I suggest that Christians, in light of the guidance of these commandments, ought to consider what we can and should do to help our nation and the nations of the earth to find the path to peace.

A besetting transgression of most faith traditions is to share theological perspectives in ways which discredit or demean others. In setting forth a negative critique of war, one may appear to be disregarding the sacrifices and positive contributions of those who are associated with the defense of our nation. Several candid acknowledgments are in order as I seek to give the strongest possible case I can against war as an instrument for achieving peace and fulfilling God's will.

We who are spared the tyranny and terror of our enemies must show respect and appreciation of those who risk their lives in the effort to defend the values we hold dear. Although he took a dim view of war, Gardner C. Taylor[1] acknowledged that "some wars must be fought. . . . I still believe the Civil War needed to be fought." As long as our nation wages war, the progressive spirit will honor the courage and commitment of our combat troops as well as conscientious objectors who find alternate ways to serve our country. No matter how vigorously we oppose war, when our country wages war, even in the face of our opposition—we are all, in a sense, at war.

We are responsible for the bullets, the bombs, and the rivers of blood. This is why citizens and their representatives must be vigilant and vigorous in demanding to be heard on matters of declarations of war. The nation that is at war is a collectivity of the consenting and the dissenting. The political triumph of one side in the debate, by virtue of national solidarity, co-opts the other in the prevailing resolve to go or not to go to war. Various levels of protest, even to the point of civil disobedience (including the willingness to accept the punishment for violations of the law), must be an option in a democratic society where the majority rules.

Harry Emerson Fosdick, founding pastor of The Riverside Church in New York City, served as a military chaplain in World War I. He experienced the horror of war and finally declared himself an unyielding pacifist. Yet he said of himself, "This does not mean that I withdrew from the manifold opportunities for public and personal usefulness in war time." He abhorred the type of pacifist "who, concerned with only keeping his own skirt lily-white, retreats from the world's problems in war time to a kind of monastic and irresponsible seclusion." [2] While denouncing war, Fosdick offered his church as a place of service for the needs of troops and their families, and a naval reserve midshipmen's school, whose headquarters were at Columbia University in New York City, was granted the opportunity to hold Vespers every Sunday evening at The Riverside Church. Often when young ensigns were ready to leave for active duty, hundreds of brides came to New York City and were married at The Riverside Church. When the war was over, the midshipmen's school had the following inscription engraved on the wall of the church:

INSCRIBED IN GRATITUDE
TO THE RIVERSIDE CHURCH
FOR ITS FRIENDLY MINISTRY
TO THE THOUSANDS OF MEN
IN TRAINING
AT THE UNITED STATES NAVAL RESERVE MIDSHIPMEN'S
SCHOOL IN THE CITY OF NEW YORK
AND FOR THE INSPIRATION
GIVEN THEM
BY THE PRIVILEGE OF WORSHIPPING
AT THE MIDSHIPMEN'S VESPER SERVICES.
MAY 1941 THROUGH NOVEMBER 1945

Fosdick had said that war is hell, yet he accepted the task of being heaven's faithful representative in the midst of the horrible nightmare of war seeking to find the path to peace. As progressive Christians criticize war, we are called upon to accept Glen H. Stassen's challenge in his book *Just Peacemaking*.[3] We have usually had to make a choice between "just-war theory" and pacifism. Now it is our task to set forth our best case for nonviolent peacemaking with justice.

But for now, we offer our critique through the Ten Commandments and follow that analysis with a discussion of authentic patriotism.

Commandment One: You shall have no other gods before me. God is the creator of us all, the supreme being and source of life. War elevates an ideology, nation, interest, or principle to the status of ultimate, life-or-death urgency and offers salvation through violence, rather than through love of God and our neighbor. War makes race, creed, class, nationality, national interest, natural resources, land, or national security into a kind of a god, putting the creature ahead of the creator. We may pray to God for success in wartime, but we should not call our military actions an act of worship unto God. We worship what we have made ultimate as justification for devastating other parts of God's creation.

Commandment Two: You shall not make for yourself an idol. An icon or image that represents people's highest values can help focus attention and make us more attentive to what we care for most deeply, but when they are worshipped in place of God, they become idols. When a nation or a people choose to elevate their ideas or interests ahead of God, they also bow down before symbols created to lead them into battles. When we allow any human-made thing to become the image upon which we hang our existence and to which we give our lives, we have made an idol. Flags, especially, are used to show our patriotism and national values. In wartime, patriotic symbols and slogans achieve an almost ultimate status. It becomes sacriligious not to bow down to them as the faithful do before the altar of God. Flags acquire a divine power that overrides and violates the core values of justice and peace, and they cast war in the soft rosy glow of patriotism so that we won't examine the killing fields behind them.

Commandment Three: You shall not make wrongful use of the name of your God. Many of us had parents who admonished us not to swear, not to "take the Lord's name in vain." "Vain" comes from Latin and means empty. That is the basis for the most common use of this commandment—the idea that taking God's name for a frivolous or angry purpose is disrespectful of what is holy, powerful, and the most important being in our lives. After all, would we use the name of someone we honor, respect, and love in a way that would be insulting to them?

"Vain" can also mean a conceited pride about personal appearance. In this sense, vanity is the false mask of war. In war, patriotism is taken in vain; we use patriotic makeup to conceal the devastations of war and make it seem noble and good. The brushes and paints of vanity are spin, public relations, and marketing, which hide the carnage and keep the grieving families out of public view. If we kill, does it thereby make it a righteous deed?

Swearing and vanity are sins (I suspect many of us have committed them in our lives), but the deeper violation of this commandment is when we use God's name to start a war, to say God wills it, or to ask God to bless a nation that goes to war. God has plainly said, "Thou shalt not kill," but when we call God's name to sanction our wars, we break a commandment. Far worse than profanity, when we use swear words to call God's name, we are betraying God, taking the name of God and surrendering it to the principalities and powers of death and destruction. To say we believe in a God of love, who upholds justice for all, who cares for all of creation and every living thing in it, and who embraces us with mercy, forgiveness, and joy, and to cry for war, to glorify it, to make it noble is to take God's name in vain.

Commandment Four: Remember the Sabbath and keep it holy. War combatants sometimes arrange a ceasefire to show respect for the Sabbath or other holy days. There is a famous World War II story about European soldiers on both sides stopping at Christmas to sing carols together while in their respective foxholes. But this was easier to do when people of one religion were fighting each other. In any case, it is hard to arrange a total Sabbath in war—a ceasefire is not the same as stopping all the machinery and strategic-planning activities of war.

In most wars, the Sabbath is ignored because no one can afford to stop the warring goals to honor it. Worse, today, the Sabbath or high holy days have become a good day to launch a surprise attack. It is very difficult to keep any times sacred in a time of war. Missiles fly in midnight skies; troops march with night goggles; tanks roll at dawn; and bullets strike human flesh on Sunday morning.

Commandment Five: Honor your Father and Mother. This commandment brings the cost of war home, to the place where it pierces the life-giving heart of every society.

Mothers and fathers give us the gift of life. Serving as God's channels of life is one of the noblest expressions of human achievement. Parents nourish us and nurture us toward health and wholeness. Parents teach values. They instruct siblings in how to get along with one another, how to resolve conflicts nondestructively, and how to share. And then along comes war. Did not our parents teach us that seeking to destroy those with whom we disagree is not civilized? Even as they taught us not to be afraid of bullies and to defend ourselves, they reprimanded us when our anger boiled over into violence against others. As parents age and reach nearer to the end of life, their greatest reward for the years of love and care and guidance and education that they have offered their children is to be respected and appreciated and to be offered care in return. This is the great circle of life. When our sons and daughters depart to fields of combat, even for love of country, they must slay the sons and daughters of some other parents and destroy this circle of life.

Deep in the hearts of mothers and fathers is a recognition that the most basic violation is when their children are slain. War steals their children, returns them broken in spirit and, often, broken in flesh. Worse, it offers their lifeless, broken bodies to be swathed in our sorrow and heartbreak and laid into the ground too soon, far too soon. The prophet Isaiah, when he described a people who lived faithful to the Lord, said that they would not work in vain and that they would not raise their children for calamity. To honor fathers and mothers is to keep their children from calamity, even from the calamity of war.

Commandment Six: You shall not kill. Most Christian

thinkers accept that sometimes we kill in self-defense or to protect our families or communities. But, even when we accept the necessity of killing to save life, we must call it a sin. Sin is separation from God and God's will for our lives. The wisdom of this commandment is that all killing separates us from God. Taking a life, even for a justifiable reason, does not nullify the fact that killing is sin. It harms everyone who is around the deceased, and the community has once again experienced failure and loss. God's love is constant. Even if the victim has been up to no good, the spirit of the community is injured by this loss. Taking a life denies grace the opportunity to bring that person to a better life and more positive outcomes of change.

Killing also harms the killer. We see this all the time with soldiers. We even have a name for it. We call it Post-traumatic Stress Disorder. We know that even the authorized killing of people by those trained to kill causes the soul great damage that needs healing to be restored to itself and to God.

The kind of killing organized by state systems is, according to many ethicists, a whole order of killing different from the personal, agonizing decisions people might have to make to protect themselves or their family. When you can see or know the victim, the ethical choice makes the decision to kill traumatic, but it also makes it possible to remember, to process, and to heal from the act and be restored to God. What does it mean, however, when we allow the state to kill on our behalf in such instances as capital punishment, undercover intelligence, and destabilization of governments with or without our knowledge, for our possible benefit, and at

our expense, even when we do not support such killing? How
are we collectively to heal and be restored to God? Usually,
nations that go to war have a hard time with such questions.
They prefer to idolize their warriors instead of healing them
or caring for the disabled and offering lifelong health care for
them. They refuse to count the lingering traumas and aftermath of war as part of the massive cost of war.

Jesus offers us insight into why this particular commandment is so violated, especially by war. At many points, he
reminds us that life is more than our flesh, more than the
sum of harm that can be inflicted on us, more than the
impact of torture, injury, or death. We have a spirit in us that
is the life of our flesh, but also transcends the life of the flesh.
That is why Jesus said to Pilate, "You can kill me, but you
have no power over me." The Bible says blasphemy of this
Spirit is the unforgivable sin. To kill the love of God, to violate the power of courage, to destroy hope in the soul—these
are ways to blaspheme the spirit. War, for all the noble language we wrap around it, is hell. We inflict it most grievously
on the young and the poor, whose spirit is the most vulnerable because the young are still growing into themselves. War
takes that youth and breaks down the love of neighbor with
hatred of the enemy, the hope for peace with the willingness
to kill, and the ordinary power of love with the adrenaline
rush of fear. War takes the Spirit of God in a person and blas-
phemes it, injuring both flesh and spirit.

Commandment Seven: You shall not commit adultery.
Most of us interpret this one literally and attach it to the
marriage contract. However, the prophets understood marriage as the relationship of covenant between God and the

people. These ancient thinkers lived, of course, in what feminists call patriarchal, or male-dominated, societies, so they tended to define adultery not as what men did, but as the misbehavior of women. We still don't have a good equivalent term for mistress—mister just doesn't have the same whiff of scandal. Now, though, I hope we can see adultery as a two-way street. Both men and women can betray covenant relationships, practice duplicity, spend money betraying others, and forfeit their integrity.

Whatever the highest and noblest values a nation claims for itself, in times of war, it must always suspend them while pretending to honor them. Married to justice, peace, truth, and the pursuit of a common good and happiness for all, a nation at war cavorts with injustice, propaganda, violence, environmental destruction, and oppression. It pursues a phantom lover, straight into a sea of blood.

Commandment Eight: You shall not steal. War does not just steal the spirits and lives of our young men and women and the hopes of their parents; it literally requires stealing from enemies. In war, people invade other people's lands, take their dignity and self-respect, rape their bodies, loot their houses, eat their crops, and take over their resources. Those resources can be children, oil, water, money, or land, or all of them together. Of course, the greatest theft is the taking of innocent lives, noncombatant women and children who are simply in the wrong place at the wrong time. This inevitable consequence of war steals not only those lives, but the future they hold.

War also steals the resources needed to provide for the citizens of the warring nations. Those who make wartime budgets usually rationalize the balancing of the budgets on the backs of the poor. Dr. King reminded us that the money sucked up from a nation by the vacuum cleaner of war leaves poverty in its wake. In this way even the aftermath of war is a continuing legacy of taking milk out of the mouths of babies.

Commandment Nine: You shall not bear false witness against your neighbor. Propaganda, disinformation, and outright lies are the stock and trade of war. We bear false witness against enemies, inventing dehumanizing names to call them, propagating distortions of their culture or beliefs, and stereotyping and creating caricatures to engender hatred. We also do the same with our fellow citizens who protest or dissent against war. It is impossible to have a war without bearing false witness. If we had to tell the truth about our enemies and ourselves, we might see how similar we are as human beings. We might have to see that we are trying to hate others like us who love their country and want a decent, good life for themselves and their children, and who long for peace when there is no peace.

Commandment Ten: You shall not covet your neighbor's house or your neighbor's wife. In times of war, we covet the neighbor's power, possessions, and life. Nations do not go to war without wanting something from their enemy and forcing their enemies to defend what they have. The worst aspect of covetousness is that it originates not from the enemy, but from our own lack, or feeling of inferiority, or insecurity. This void or voracious longing in ourselves can never be filled by taking from others what is theirs. Hence, covetousness can never be alleviated by war, even as it fuels wars.

Nations do not go to war without wanting something

which belongs to their enemies or forcing their enemies to defend what they have. A review of the wars we have known can be explained by determining what was coveted and by whom. Was it power, control, a throne, oil, water, gold, respect, a mountain, a river, arms, women, land, or even sacred objects like a holy grail, the ark of the covenant, or a certain place of worship?

The worst aspect of covetousness is that it originates, not from the enemy, but from our own lack or feeling of deprivation or insecurity. Such a voracious longing in ourselves can never be filled by taking from others what is theirs. Persons have even been so driven that they dare to covet the authority of God. Covetousness can never be alleviated by war, because it is more frequently the impulse which fuels wars.

We must remember that civilian women experience the devastations of war. It is only recently that international legal experts have found ways to define and prosecute rape as a war crime. For centuries, and certainly in Moses's time, armies humiliated their opponents by raping or kidnapping their women. If a woman wasn't kidnapped but became pregnant, she might be killed because she had been dishonored and was regarded as shameful. If she was kidnapped as a spoil of war, she would have to serve her people's enemies for the rest of her life. We have heard tragic stories about such crimes in our own time, so we should never think about war without remembering the crimes done to women. This commandment has been broken by every war in our lifetime and by probably every war in history.

The Ten Commandments call Christians to a stricter standard about war than theories of just-war. War violates all

Ten Commandments. Some people think of them as a little old fashioned and others think the list of "thou shalt nots" are too negative. For those who like positive thinking, if a society ever took the commandments seriously, we might have peace, or at least be closer to peace.

PROPHETIC PATRIOTISM

Every Christian is called to consider the cost of war for all, even those who support a war. People of conscience can differ on whether a war is just or unjust, and not every Christian, even a progressive Christian, is a pacifist. Some believe that wars are sometimes necessary, but they should be extremely rare. Christian faith should compel us to be honest, however, about the cost of war—and the Ten Commandments remind us of what is at stake when nations go to war. Clergy are among those who most clearly know the cost of war because its victims and their families sit in our pews. We live close to the truths of war, and it is our obligation not to lie from the pulpit, not to violate the Ten Commandments. Without this truth telling, we will abandon the sacred calling of all Christians to be peacemakers and forget that peace itself is not a quick or easy solution to the world's problems. Peace, too, is very costly.

We call for peace, but we must calculate carefully what kind of peace we seek. A shallow truce, a ceasefire, a withdrawal, these may signal an end to war, but they must not be confused with the presence of peace. The lasting peace to which Jesus Christ calls us will cost each and every one of us. It is not the same cost as the trillions spent on war. The cost of peace has a different calculation. To renew our hope for peace, we must discern what we may do for the high cost of peace.

We must forfeit the cycle of violence, fear, greed, revenge, and hate that propels us from one war to the next. We must abandon our idols, our false witness, our covetousness, our betrayals of covenant, and all the profits we accrue from fighting and winning wars. We must take the risks of living in a new way—not just personally, not just in our churches, cities, and country, but in the world. When He called for peace, Jesus Christ had paid a dear price, his life. Knowing that God is trustworthy to see us all through any trial the world can inflict and having yielded himself into the hands of God, Jesus had great authority to say, "Peace be unto you." But that peace was purchased at the price of a life that was dedicated and committed to achieving it. That can be the high cost of peace.

Jesus also said, "Receive you the Holy Spirit." Most Christians will not have to pay with their lives for peace, and, if we are honest, we must say that many of us, if we are threatened, behave like anyone else who is scared. We run away or find some weapon to fight the assault. Human cowardice and fear are why we need to heed Jesus's admonition, "Receive the Spirit." A fundamental responsibility of Christian ministry is to teach and to preach this Spirit and help a community embody this Spirit. The Spirit Jesus offers must convince us that we can trust God and entrust ourselves in God's keeping and the community of faith that God has ordained. Such spiritual revitalization is central to the prospect of a new quality of life in this nation and the whole of the world.

There is one more responsibility for peace, and it is the most difficult. Jesus said, "To those of you who are my body, who have been filled with my spirit, whose sins, you forgive on earth will be forgiven them. And whose sins you retain shall be retained" (John 20:22–23 NRSV). He is saying you cannot get into heaven unless those you have hurt give you a letter of reference. Those you hurt determine whether or not you belong in heaven, and you cannot get there unless your enemy releases you. That is awful—I don't think many of us really want to believe that this is the truth—for it suggests that we cannot get to heaven unless Iraqi insurgents say so— and that they cannot get there unless we say so. This might cause some Christians to panic. Help! Help!

"Peace be unto you." That is what Jesus said. On the heels of this comment, at another gathering two weeks later, he said the same thing, "Peace, peace. Peace be unto you." Many now would agree with the word that he said and the blessing it offered: yes, it is time for peace. But what is the price of peace? We must work for moral and spiritual revital- ization. We must restore love and the spirit to our relation- ship with God and our relationships to each other and we must pursue what I call "prophetic patriotism."

Most people do not just want to hang around in life, just work, eat, and die without a purpose, without having made a mark in the world, without having their lives matter to oth- ers. The same is also true of a people, a nation. Hence, we may ask: what is the purpose, the vocation of the United States, and how can prophetic patriotism help us achieve that purpose? Prophetic patriotism is based on the conviction that God has a good purpose for the nation, but it carries the recognition that God did not ordain from the foundation of the world that we would be a holy commonwealth of liberty and justice, no matter what we do. Prophetic patriots believe that our keeping faith with God's purpose brings fulfillment to the nation—if we do justly, right will come to us. Prophetic patriots are convinced that the quality of the lives of the people is a measure of the society. America is not great, right or wrong. No! Prophetic patriotism says, if we do not pray and work for the well-being of all, if we turn from our God and are not living according to the ways of God's word, which is peace, which is justice, and which is love, even this nation will perish from the earth. These three elements, peace, justice, and love, tell us God's purpose for the nation. If we live out that purpose, we shall be fulfilled.

Dr. Edwina Hunter,[4] a retired professor of preaching, tells a story from a time when she was a teacher in Kentucky, when the nation was engaged in another unpopular, controversial war in Asia. She was in charge of a group that was putting on a drama and she had left them to get things ready for the performance. While she was busy on her own tasks, someone called her and said, "You better watch out because I think somebody is going to come and serve a summons on you." "What for?" she asked. The caller told her to go and see what her students were up to.

When she got to the theater, she saw that for the stage backdrop, some students had hung the flag upside down. Another of the students had gone to a local judge and complained that there was desecration intended in the play that night, signified by that flag. Hunter talked to the students. She said, "I will not tell you what to do, but I want to know why you have turned the flag upside down."

The students' answer is instructive for us today. One student in the group explained that when a ship at sea is in distress, the colors are turned upside down. Their point was well taken; their nation was troubled. Prophetic patriotism understands that when a nation is in distress, heading for hard times and difficult days, and its policies no longer reflect the heart of its vocation, someone had better find the courage to hang its flag upside down. Prophetic patriotism values the symbol of the flag, but does not make it an idol. Instead, it understands how powerfully the effective use of a symbol can capture the truth of what lies behind it.

I am not recommending we turn flags upside down, burn them, or refuse to say the Pledge of Allegiance. What I hope for are people who understand the meaning of prophetic patriotism. These are the people who understand that when God loves us, we must be open to God telling us the truth about our situation. In Jesus, God reveals that we are capable of destroying the very one who came to give us life. Those of us who gather at the table with Jesus must remember that we have not been nearly as patriotic as we ought to have been for the Kingdom of God. However, God loves us and calls us. Come, come again and again and again, until the love at the table is deep in our hearts, and, out of that love, we can go forth and love our nation, calling it back to its rightful vocation. Let us go forth to the nation and speak a word of challenge until our nation truly becomes America the beautiful, America the land of peace, "under God with justice for all."

Critique, Confession, and Ecological Consciousness

M artin Luther King Jr. spoke of the faith community as too often being the tail lights instead of the head lights of social change. Such is the case with the ecological movement. Despite some lone theological voices crying in the wilderness for decades,[1] and more recent "creation care" and other environmental movements of evangelicals and progressives, the hard truth is that *An Inconvenient Truth*, a documentary by former vice president Al Gore, did more to capture our attention regarding global warming and the environmental crisis than all the sermons preached from our nation's pulpits in recent years. With rare exceptions secular voices have taken the lead in sounding the alarm about how certain trends in our technological society are already imperiling life on this beautiful blue planet we call home.

THE ECOLOGICAL CRISIS

There was a time when the abundance of space, natural resources, and access to essential goods made it appear that there was no limit to what we could obtain and enjoy. Ours was the Promised Land, "flowing with milk and honey," as the Bible says. For such abundance we gave thanks and consumed all we desired without any thought for future reserves. As the population grew we became aware that not everyone had even the basic necessities. Serious inequities existed in the distribution of resources, but when the poor lack adequate resources, their destitution is generally viewed as a matter of their laziness, irresponsibility, or bad luck. Since there is enough for everyone, they need only work hard to obtain it. With the advent of the industrial revolution, mechanization, and mass production, we came to believe that with unlimited resources and technological know-how, scarcity could become a thing of the past. The science of productivity is such that we only have to define the problem and, in a very short time, the solution will appear.

But a strange thing has happened on the way to "infinite growth and productivity." We have learned that the soil that produces our crops and supplies raw materials for our giant factories will be depleted if mistreated. We also have discovered that industrial processes produce waste which, when dumped into our rivers and streams, contaminates our water and soil. And when contaminants are spewed forth from smokestacks, the air becomes polluted. They foul the soil and the streams, kill the fish, pollute drinking water, and make people sick. Meanwhile petroleum-based production and use releases more carbon into the air; carbon dioxide traps heat and ultraviolet rays in our atmosphere and causes the greenhouse effect. Altered weather patterns contribute to an increase of violent storms. Global warming, melting of the polar cap, and the general rise of coastal waters lead to the increase of debilitating conditions affecting the quality of life on our planet. Emissions of chlorofluorocarbons help to deplete the ozone layer and make us more vulnerable to ultraviolet rays. And shortages are beginning to develop in petro-fuels and safe drinking water. Poverty induces an increase in the use of trees for fuel and adds to the problem of deforestation and desertification, which contributes to the destruction of species.

We already see signs that all of our progress that we so proudly pursued may have brought us to a tipping point where the negative trends become irreversible. We are close to crossing the line where we will be too late to stop the permanently compromised viability and sustainability of planet earth. Various environmental authorities debate how close we are to that irreversible disaster zone. Yet we do not have to await the conclusions from the debates among the scientific experts. Violent and unpredictable weather, fluctuating oil prices, erosion of soil, food costs, scarcity of both oil and water, health epidemics, and other destabilizations in natural cycles we had learned to take for granted—all these sound the alarm. This is no time for foolishness.

Perhaps an insight from human development may offer a clue to what has happened to us. The gift of life at its start is filled with vitality and promises of unimaginable possibilities. One of the characteristics of youth is the feeling of invulnerability and the tendency to seize the moment without assessing the future consequences. It is not a matter of "enjoy now, pay later" but rather "now is the golden moment and the golden coin has already been paid by adults." Whole societies can sometimes be plagued by this kind of adolescence, remaining unrestrained in consumption and not counting up the cost and paying the price.

Or perhaps a better explanation comes from the biblical story of Noah. God had warned him that a mighty flood was coming. God instructed him to build an ark to secure humans and animals during the deluge. Noah preached about his project and admonished the people to get ready. Because there was not a cloud in the sky and nobody could remember when they had experienced even scattered showers, he became the laughingstock, "the crazy man" of the community. Parents took their kids to see a man building a boat when there was no water for miles around. In the course of time, however, it began to rain, hard. After forty days of constant rain, the flood waters began rising, and it became clear that unforeseen disaster was upon the skeptics. Our lives are impacted by events so far in the distant past that we could not possibly have seen what was coming. Still, our actions today will determine the survival of generations yet to come.

Prophets are called seers because they are given the long view and they help us face the present moment in the light of eternity. Great cultures honor and preserve wisdom that can only be remembered by the mountains and the mighty waters of the sea. Native American traditions seek to offer prophetic wisdom when they encourage us to think in terms of the "seventh generation." Chief Seattle's counsel was captured by Ted Perry in the words:

This we know,
All things are connected

like the blood
which unites one's family . . .
Whatever befalls the earth,
befalls the sons and daughters of the earth.
Man did not weave the web of life;
he is merely a strand in it.
Whatever he does to the web,
he does to himself.
   —Ted Perry, inspired by Chief Seattle[2]

This prophetic insight is grounded in reverence and respect for nature and an awareness of the interrelatedness of all orders of creation. It functions out of an if-then sensibility. There are consequences to all our actions—for us and for generations to come. Disrespect for the earth and a disregard for the counsel of the elders and the Great Spirit will lead to great peril for the people. If we listen and observe, we will be instructed about what brings harmony and well-being and also what foreshadows disaster and death.

Thinking with respect and awareness for the orders of creation seems "inconvenient" in a world of a diminished sense of the sacred. Our society has a strong leaning toward materialism and commodification. We swagger with a thoughtless confidence in unlimited resources and a sense of the inevitability of progress. We have an egocentric fascination with our own power to create what we need through our technological genius and an addiction to pleasure and instant gratification. Numerous historical analyses and political, sociological, and economic studies help us understand how the culture came to hold the values of our time, values that have brought us to the point of ecological crisis. According to some critics, one contributing factor is found in certain biblical and theological understandings of Judeo-Christian faith.

Even more disturbing than our ineffectual witness for environmental responsibility are these charges that the church may indeed be a major culprit in promoting values and a mind-set that seem to support the assault against earth, air, and water. Many conscientious believers are not even aware that some of our strongest convictions may have contributed to the ecological crisis being discussed these days.

Certain religious understandings have helped to fuel the destructive machinery of rapacious consumption and utter disregard of the earth, its nonhuman inhabitants, and the atmosphere that envelops all of us. They ignore the signs of disease and destruction that are already impacting our quality of life and moving us toward a calamitous situation. From time to time, companies issue a factory recall for products they have placed on the market when it becomes clear that there is a design defect hazardous to consumers. As we look at the evidence provided by environmentalists, we are long overdue in issuing a massive factory recall because of our defective and hazardous religious way of viewing the world.

ANTI-ECOLOGICAL TENDENCIES IN THE CHURCH

Let us identify what some of these perspectives are and how they may have contributed to the problem. Until we understand the problem, we will not be able to see what positive tenets from the Judeo-Christian worldview will help move us toward a transformative response to our environmental crises. With careful examination, we will also find insights in our faith tradition that may help energize us not only to see things differently but also to act upon the wisdom we have received from other learned and experienced quarters.

We have anti-ecological tendencies that encourage harming the environment. We also have positive principles that we have misinterpreted, so that we have drifted into an anti-ecological mind-set and distorted our ability to understand divine intent. Consider the following ways of thinking:

First of all, the human-centric view sees the other orders of creation as of no intrinsic value, but of only instrumental benefit to us. We stand at the center of the universe surrounded by all these things made just for us. All the billions of years of the evolution of the world were a preparatory phase awaiting our arrival as human beings. Until we stood erect as Homo sapiens, meaning and purpose were merely waiting in the wings. Of course, this way of speaking is not to be found in chapter and verse of our holy writings. But the Bible is often used to support an idea that we want to believe but the Bible does not directly address. Because we think of God as our heavenly parent, humanity as favored children, and the universe as our nursery, we developed an egocentric mindset. Like an infant in a cradle, inclined to see the whole world as existing for his or her comfort and well-being, we have a tendency to see the universe as a birthday gift from God, just for us.

The first book of the Bible does explicitly give humankind a prime role in the continuation of creation. Genesis 1:26 bestows special status on us: And God said, "Let us make humankind in our image, according to our likeness, and let them have dominion over the fish of the sea and over the birds of the air, and over the cattle, and over all the wild animals of the earth, over every creeping thing that creeps upon the earth." We have interpreted the "dominion" granted to humankind as giving us raw power to exploit and abuse the rest of creation, rather than as requiring mature responsibility of us to show respect and loving care for creation.

Like rebellious adolescents, we have been inclined to see the gifts of God as ours to use as we choose. God has promised abundance so we neglect to preserve or conserve. We think of God's providential care as meaning that all our needs will be provided for and that there are no limits to what we may consume. In the face of scarcity, we are encouraged to have the confidence that God will make miraculous provision for us. Some of our most beloved and familiar passages of scripture have contributed to an expectation of miraculous provision. For example, in the book of Exodus, quail and insect secretions arrive like manna from heaven and sustain the Israelites. Or we use the account in Luke of a sudden abundance of fish squirming out of the nets that had previously come up empty, convincing Simon, James, and John to follow Jesus. How easily we ignore the second message of the Exodus incident—not only did God provide for the Israelites who had fled to the wilderness, but also the people were instructed not to hoard this natural resource but to use only as much as was needed and no more. We also think of the Promised Land as having an unlimited flow of milk and honey: "a land where you may eat bread without scarcity, where you will lack nothing, a land whose stones are iron and from whose hills you may mine copper. You shall eat your fill and bless the Lord your God for the good land that [God] has given you" (Deuteronomy 8:9–10).

Even as we revel in the idea of God sending us unlimited material blessings, we espouse a dualism in which spiritual reality is of primary significance and material things are of secondary importance. The spiritual dimensions of life are eternal and of a higher purpose while the earth will eventually pass away, making material concerns ephemeral and unspiritual. According to this understanding, we need not revere and respect earth, air, or water, and we can treat our bodies as expendable, paying more attention to the soul. However, in ignoring the importance of the physical context which sustains our biological existence, we also undermine the capacity of our bodies to sustain mental, emotional, and spiritual health. In fact, the spiritual and the material are beneficial to each other in a mutual and complementary relationship. The attempt to separate one from the other is a distortion of the nature of life; taken together, they are a truer reflection of reality.

When we are threatened with the possibility of the mass destruction of the earth, we expect divine intervention to provide an alternative safe haven—even a new heaven and a new earth. Or, in the secular version of this myth, if we destroy the air and water and run out of food, we will have already discovered another planet more bountiful than the one we would have exhausted. Such ideologies, both in their religious and secular forms, justify callous indifference to the well-being of the earth's biosphere.

Even as we place humankind at the pinnacle of creation

as masters of everything, we also divide up human beings through our maldistribution of resources. The wealthy live on an island of affluence in a sea of poverty. Indifference to vast economic disparities is justified as God's wrath against those who suffer from impoverishment. Those "predestined to decay will perish," whereas there will always be plenty for God's elect, a theology that gives people with the means to help others an excuse to ignore the maldistribution of resources. We are the chosen.

A GREENER THEOLOGY

The cosmic cry of nature protests these anti-ecological and anti-creation tendencies. Our neighbors in the universe— Brother Sun and Sister Moon, Brothers Wind and Air, in the words of St. Francis of Assisi—are crying out in effect, "C'mon, y'all." Thousands of years ago the psalmist declared, "The heavens are telling the glory of God; and the firmament proclaims [God's] handiwork. Day to day pours forth speech, and night to night declares knowledge. There is no speech, nor are there words; their voice is not heard; yet their voice goes out through all the earth and their words to the end of the world" (Psalm 19:1–4). The heavens are crying now as we erode the ozone layer and invite irreversible destruction upon God's good creation, exhaust precious natural resources, and defile the space we share with our neighbors in the universe.

Let us hope it is not too late to heed the call of the Spirit. Let us seize the option and opportunities to reverse our negative tendencies. Even as scientists work feverishly to better understand how to halt and reverse the damage, even as environmentalists in the "green revolution" are advancing common sense changes in behavior and encouraging us to reuse, refuse, and recycle, even as businesses and industries are developing everything from "green" buildings to hybrid vehicles, even as world leaders make steps toward global agreements and commitments that set limits on carbon emissions and other environmental damage, we religious leaders must do our part to correct the distorted theologies and ideologies that have contributed to the destruction of our environment and begin to build a "greener" theology to guide us in a sustainable life for all of creation.

Let us remember that from the beginning creation was good. Throughout the biblical account of the origins of the world, we read again and again, "And God saw that it was good." However metaphorical the biblical account of creation may be, its essence is how we must appreciate and care for the earth. We have to value the earth as God's good creation instead of ravaging it to meet our insatiable longings. We must stop mindlessly lopping off the tops of mountains to strip-mine for coal or casually dumping toxins into the waters. When I look at human beings, I see "handmade by God" stamped on each forehead, and I believe that every aspect of the created order has the same stamp "handmade by God" on it. Therefore, creation cannot be disrespected or disregarded or taken as of only instrumental value for us.

In Genesis 1:28, God instructed humanity, male and female, to "fill the earth and subdue it; and have dominion over the fish of the sea and over the birds of the air and over every living thing that moves upon the earth." While the Hebrew word for "subdue," *kabas*, has negative, even violent or coercive implications, the notion of dominion holds great promise for a more ecological theology. Dominion, or sovereignty, is derived from the Latin word *dominus*, or "lord." There is a difference between dominion and domination. As ones created in God's image, we must care for creation as God does. But God does not waste, damage, squander, or pollute. God preserves, heals, conserves, and tends. Rather than seeing ourselves as mandated to exercise absolute power over other creatures and the earth, we need to recall and reclaim a notion of stewardship that entails responsibility, care, preservation, and maximization of what there is for the long haul. As I was walking down the street the other day, I saw a wrecking company truck with a sign on the side, and I thought, good stewardship should not be a matter of our being hired to be the "wrecking crew" of creation. As good stewards, we must be priests and prophets of the earth.

Priests have a responsibility to guide good Sabbath practices. We must reclaim our understanding of Sabbath—a time to step back, as did God on the seventh day, and appreciate the goodness of creation. We desperately need a time-out from the relentless pace of earning and spending and consuming and bankruptcy and financial hassles. If Christians re-embrace the concept of Sabbath as a time of rest, a time to cultivate relationships with God and neighbors and a profound respectfulness for all, perhaps we could reclaim a reverence for life. In the book of Exodus, Moses reminded the people that the Sabbath was not only set aside for the good of humankind, but also for all of life. "Six days you shall do your work, but on the seventh day you shall rest, so that your ox and your donkey may have relief, and your home born slave and the resident alien may be refreshed" (Exodus 23:12). This sense of the Sabbath as for all of life is reinforced in the biblical idea of a Sabbath year for fields, "You shall let [the land] rest and lie fallow, so that the poor of your people may eat; and what they leave the wild animals may eat" (Exodus 23:11a).

The Psalmist proclaims, "The earth is the Lord's and the fullness thereof" (Psalm 24). Only a criminal or someone mentally deranged would thoughtlessly walk into a stranger's home and eat through their cupboards leaving only crumbs behind, clog the sink with trash, uproot the ficus tree in the pot in the corner and the plant on the table, and run through a pack of cigarettes, filling the house with smoke. We consider it criminal to treat someone else's home in such a destructive manner. Moses reminded the people that "the heaven and the heaven of heavens belong to the Lord your God, the earth with all that is in it," before continuing to reiterate how God expected the people to live. Not only is the creation good, as declared by God, but it also belongs to *God*, not us. How dare we treat as trash what is God's treasure?

Woven throughout the biblical witness, especially in Leviticus and Deuteronomy, are instructions and limits for the Israelites in how they are to treat animals and the earth, from the Sabbath instructions for every seventh year to less familiar regulations. In Deuteronomy, there are instructions for preserving the trees and wildlife. (Deuteronomy 20:19: "You must not destroy [a captured town's] trees by wielding an ax against them. Although you may take food from them, you must not cut them down." Deuteronomy 22:6: "If you come on a bird's nest, in any tree or on the ground, with fledglings or eggs, and the mother sitting on [them] . . . let the

mother go . . . in order that it may go well with you and you
may live long.") God did not intend for us to treat the earth
and the animals in an unthinking and needlessly destructive
manner but to exercise restraint, fairness, and compassion,
and to maintain resources for the future. Throughout, these
limits reflect a divine concern for the big picture. Divine
instructions are for the good of the individuals who live by
themselves, for their neighbors, for the disadvantaged—
whether the poor, the captive, or the stranger—for future
generations, and for the earth and its nonhuman creatures.
What a contrast to our single-minded focus on what we want
for ourselves right now!

When we seriously engage in a conversation with and
about God and ecology, it may play havoc with traditional
notions of the nature of God. The way we relate to the environment tests our sense of what God's nature is all about. If,
as Genesis claims, the Spirit of God was breathed on all that
exists, then the universe and the evolution of life become the
handiwork of God's Spirit. Evolution, especially, shows how
interconnected all life is and how the divine spirit of creativity permeates all of creation and creates life through the
reality of relationality. Pantheism holds that the total of
everything *is* God; panentheism understands everything as
being *in* God, but that a dimension of God transcends and
relates to creation. God is male, female, principle of being,
energy of being, end of being, matrix of being, but also more.
How we treat God's world, how we treat God's people and
how we treat God's earth reveal to us how we view God and
what we consider to be our relationship to the world.

Ecology is a panentheistic theology because it points to

the centrality of relationality—and not simply human relationality. The ecological movement isn't just about saving our hides, and abundant life isn't just about having more stuff. Abundance of life is a perspective that affirms how multifaceted and multilayered is our actual participation in life. A faithful approach to ecology recognizes a mystical dynamic of spirit and a yes to God's invitation to join as co-creators beyond the scientific urgency of our current crises.

In Romans 8, Paul reminds us that the whole creation is waiting to be set free from its bondage to decay and to obtain the freedom of the glory of the children of God. Thus he links our longing for redemption to that for which creation itself is groaning. In this way of thinking, the universe is not just the protective enclosure for our human strivings or the commissary for obtaining our nutritional and other biological necessities. We are partners in hope together. Whatever redemption we hope for ourselves, we join the other aspects of creation in prayerful expectation and longing. We do not speak the same language as plants, animals, or the cosmic bodies. But there must be resonance between God and every creature God has made. That Jesus spoke to the wind that stirred the raging sea, we think of as metaphor or miracle. But there is a universal language of love not cramped into our limited linguistic modes of expression. Later in Romans 8, Paul tells us that the Spirit understands the longings of our hearts even when we are limited to sighs and groans too deep for words. St. Francis of Assisi and St. Benedict of Nursia affirmed our capacity in the Spirit to have I-Thou relationships beyond our own species. What a different way of life we would experience if we really believed the words of Psalm 19,

"The heavens are telling the glory of God; and the firmament proclaims [God's] handiwork. Day to day pours forth speech, and night to night declares knowledge. There is no speech, nor are there words; their voice is not heard; yet their voice goes out through all the earth, and their words to the end of the world" (Psalm 19:1–4). After hearing Joseph Haydn's stirring anthem *The Heavens Are Telling*, it seemed appropriate to inquire about the message the heavens sought to share with us. This is what I experienced and the song I wrote in response to my question:

Song of the Heavens

What are the heavens telling us?
What truth does the cosmos convey?
What intimations are found in creation?
The sounds and the silences,
What do they say?

(Chorus)
The heavens are saying we all are one—
The earth, the sky, and the stars above
When we care for one another
As sister, as brother,
We glorify our God who created us for love.

Ponder the union of time and space
Observe how the galaxies dance.
Some species flourish that others be nourished
Could such cosmic synergy be only chance?

(Chorus)

This is the call of the Universe:
Behold what a wonder are we
Love is the mystery shaping our destiny
Weaving connections of all things that be.

(Chorus)[3]

WHERE DO WE GO FROM HERE?

In Jeremiah 18, God tells the prophet to observe a potter making a vessel. The vessel was marred in the potter's hand, so the potter mashed the clay down again to make the vessel as it was intended to be. Drawing insight from this image, the prophet advises his people what they should do. They are told to turn from their evil and to amend their ways and their doings and reshape themselves according to divine justice and mercy. Similarly, in our times we are called to face and fix the flaws of our misinterpreted faith and our misguided life practices. We are called today to remake ourselves anew.

Now that we know the transgressions involved in our behavior, we can no longer consider such behavior to be just idiosyncratic mistakes, but a manifestation of our sinfulness. We must call our polluting, contaminating, wasteful, and consuming ways for what they are—evil. As we name the evil we must call our world to confession and repentance about our ecological transgressions. We must address and confess the flaws in our understanding about the environment. We must be proactive in our witness and become the new "abolitionists" in regard to ecological oppression. We must ask for forgiveness and seek the pardon of any cosmic component that we have unwittingly offended. Through the arts, poetry, musical gifts, and our daily endeavors, we should apologize. Where we have disrespected sun, moon, stars, land, air, or water, we should prepare rituals in which we earnestly seek forgiveness. Rachel Carson, in *Silent Spring*, the classic work that launched the environmental movement, enumerates the specific contaminating behaviors that should be on our list of transgressions we need to confess. As we seek forgiveness, we must also learn to listen for a reply.

In 1949, the popular thought concerning the role of the elements in our environment was often ill-defined, as we hear in the words of songs such as "Ol' Man River" and "That Lucky Old Sun." Haven Gillespie and Beasley Smith's "That Lucky Old Sun"—which was performed and recorded by many people, including Frankie Laine, Frank Sinatra, Louis Armstrong, Ray Charles, and Willie Nelson—entertained us with the notion that the sun was oblivious to the workings of the real world.

> Up in the morning, out on the job, work like the devil
> for my pay,
> lucky old sun, ain't got nothing to do, roll around
> heaven all day.
> Dear Lord above, can't you see I'm cryin', tears are in
> my eyes.
> Send down a cloud with a silver lining, take me to
> paradise.

> Show me that river, lead me across, and take all my
>   troubles away.
> Like the lucky old sun, I'll have nothing to do but roll
>   around heaven all day.

The song suggests that unlike us humans the sun has nothing
to do but roll around heaven all day. Of course artists engage
in hyperbole or use metaphor or allegory to achieve a star-
tling effect in pointing to an aspect of the truth, but now that
we are aware of how much we are all dependent upon the
constancy of the sun's gift to all the universe and to our galaxy
in particular, I think some of us might owe the sun an apol-
ogy. The sun in some traditions becomes an image of God;
we may be insulting our creator as well. The constancy of
God's love may not be noticed, but without it we cease to be.
The sun warms the earth, nourishes all life, provides the light
so that we can see, and lights up the planets in our sky.

 We should undertake a massive project of sharing truth
and seeking commitment to a new way of life. We must
become experts in helping people know the truth and then to
act upon the truth they discover. The church needs to figure
out what helps people act on what they know and the wisdom
that they gain. For instance, we know pollution is bad and
conservation is good—but how do we increase the likeli-
hood that knowledge leads to better stewardship? What can
the church say to a culture? How do we change behaviors to
fit values? There is enough uncontested information about
the damage that is being done to the earth—what is the
pedagogy for faithful response to the truth we know about
our relationship to creation? In addition to new theories of

ecological spirituality, we must set forth a new praxis of environmental responsibility.

It is time for a cultural revolution of our understanding of where we stand in the universe. Just as Copernicus liberated us from an earth-centered concept of the universe to a solar-centric concept, we need to be decentered from our preconceived place of priority in the universe. We must build a cosmic fellowship of reconciliation and overcome the clash of cosmic entities. In First Corinthians 12, Paul admonishes us that the Christian community should be understood as a body where the suffering or rejoicing of one member is a shared experience. So, too, the universe is a body where the well-being of one component is related to the shalom[4] of the whole. At the heart of our faith should be a radical relationality. When asked once by a reporter whether I considered myself to be a radical, my answer was "I view myself as a 'radical relationist' with a rectifying and reconciling spirit." At this time, particularly, we must institute training of our young people to become mature cosmic citizens, training them to become radical relationists with a rectifying and reconciling spirit.

We should always require, when using our technological expertise for exploration and experimentation, a comprehensive environmental impact study. Our advanced technology brings with it an increased responsibility to study as best we can the effects of the actions we take and the innovations that we call progress. Without impact studies, what at first blush appears to be progress could be the kiss of death, the beginning of the end of our well-being.

The literature of those who oppose the eco-justice movement reveals that the driving forces behind their research and their findings are productivity and economic gain. Indeed, some make it very clear that their work is in service of preserving their sacred free enterprise system and economic advantages. The prospect of gain distorts even the terms of scientific discovery. Research so frequently is in service of increased riches. Therefore, we must develop specialized education that liberates people from egocentrism and greed and that allows us to move to interdependence and gratitude. Eco-justice requires us to see that sacrifice and generosity may provide the fulfillment and joy that our souls seek and need.

We need a paradigm shift from adversarial and exploitative relationships with our environment to a respectful and mutually regarding care for one another—both interspecies and intraspecies. Learning to love our neighbors in the whole ecosystem is the order of the day. It is time to expand our understanding of the Great Commandment to include love of our neighbors next door and an embrace of the whole cosmos as well. We must also renew our desire to know our universe, not for economic gain but for greater closeness to God. Knowing the Spirit of God in creation brings us closer to the created order of God of which we are only a part.

On the Sunday that I was completing this chapter, I read in the *New York Times* a paid ad informing President Obama that his emphasis on global warming was mistaken. The ad was signed by very responsible and respected scholars and leaders in business. In the face of such resistance to change, progressive Christians have an urgent responsibility to lift the issue of ecology above and beyond mere scientific research to the spiritual meaning and power of caring for creation. Beyond the reports and data, there are enduring spiritual principles that guide us which are not based on scientific findings alone. Whether the globe is warming or cooling down, our ecological sensitivity carries a humble acknowledgment that we are beneficiaries of all other elements of life in creation, and therefore, we seek to be benefactors of that life in the spirit of the Golden Rule.

In kinship with all of life and all people of faith, I have come to enjoy, especially, an ecological sensibility found in the Sufi tradition of Islam. Their story of a traveling stream gives us an ecological message about how earth, air, sun, and water are partners in hope. The tale begins with a little stream that wanted to cross the desert. But each time it tried to cross, it was swallowed up by the hot desert sand. One day the stream heard a voice saying, "Little stream, you can cross the desert." The stream asked, "How is it possible for me to cross?" The voice said, "Give yourself to the wind and it will take you across." So the stream yielded itself to the wind, which carried it across the desert and deposited it drop by drop as rain at the foot of a distant mountain. Working together, the neighbors of water, earth, air, and sun fulfilled hope. As the "Song of the Heavens" suggests what a different life we will have when we learn to heed the words of the universe: "When we care for one another as sister and brother, we glorify our God who created us for love."

Epilogue:
Trusting God Enough to "Go Forth"[1]

An unmistakable mark of interfaith sophistication for Christians is to speak of themselves as members of the Abrahamic tradition. Jews, Christians, and Muslims call Abraham the father of their faiths. We trace our religious heritage back to Abraham, the courageous man from Ur of the Chaldeans who was called by God to leave behind country, kindred, and his father's house to go forth to a land that would later be shown to him (Genesis 12:1). Along with God's call there was also an extraordinary promise:

"I will make of you a great nation, and I will bless you, and make your name great, so that you will be a blessing. I will bless those who bless you, and the one who curses you I will curse; and in you all the families of the earth shall be blessed" (Genesis 12:2–3).

The very next verse says, "So Abraham went, as the Lord had told him. . . ." (Genesis 12:4). Thus begins a journey that now includes three of the major religions of the world. Ours is a faith that offers great promises of peace, joy, justice, wholeness, meaning, purpose, community, abundant life on earth and an eternal place of rest when our journey ends here below. As was the case with Abraham, those of us who desire to experience the sublime satisfaction of being blessed and also to be a channel of God's blessings to others will be called to move beyond the cozy comforts of the familiar and the contentment of safe havens of guaranteed security. When we hear the call to let go of what we have known to venture into the realm of the unknown, what will we do? Will we be secure enough to go forth as Abraham did without a AAA TripTik or MapQuest? I ask this question of you, but I also ask it of myself. I know there is more in God's plan for me to do in order to be blessed and to be a blessing. I have even heard the call to "go forth." The words of Isaiah 54:2–4 feel like more than just a scripture reading for daily devotions. It keeps on showing up on my spiritual e-mail and my existential Facebook.

> Enlarge the site of your tent, and let the curtains
> of your habitations be stretched out; do not hold back;
> lengthen your cords and strengthen your stakes.
> For you will spread out to the right and to the left,
> and your descendants will possess the nations
> and will settle the desolate towns (Isaiah 54:2–3).

After fifty years of ministry as a pastor and professor, serving in well-established congregations and institutions of higher education, it was an Abrahamic challenge to be asked to go forth and form an institution to call citizens of the nations to see themselves as leaves of healing from the tree of life. As a leaf, people will be encouraged to be conscientious about their own health—body, mind, spirit, emotions, relationships, vocation, community relatedness, and environmental respect and responsibility. Because leaves not only nourish the plants of which they are a part, but also produce oxygen as a by-product of photosynthesis—to be a leaf is also to be intentional in being a healing influence toward others. My response to this calling has not been as immediate as Father Abraham's; it has taken time to get my mind, body, and spirit fully ready to accept the call. As a result of reviewing Abraham's story, I am now moving with a greater sense of urgency and confidence because the call keeps coming to "go forth" with a ministry of healing. The Healing of the Nations Foundation is a venture of faith in response to the call of God. The promise accompanying the call was that as I allow myself to be led by God in this work; I will know for certain that I have made a significant contribution toward fulfilling the dream of the Creator. Are you getting signals about charting a new course, breaking out of constricting places of attitude and thinking, taking on a new challenge, discovering new dimensions in your present assignment, or packing up your things for some kind of undisclosed destination? What kind of courage will it take for you to join the Abraham pilgrimage?

In re-reading the Abraham story, Genesis: 12–25, I have done some serious exegesis, even consulting my favorite commentaries on Genesis by Gerhard Von Rad[2] and Walter Brueggemann.[3] I have discovered some important clues regarding the kind of courage that will empower us to go forth to embrace God's plan for our lives. The summary statement of my findings is this: the courage to "go forth" as a part of God's plan comes from a relationship with God which enables us to: 1) experience God's call to service, 2) engage in intimate dialogue with God, and 3) trust God's faithfulness and power to provide what has been promised. Let's review some of the highlights of the Abraham narrative which reveal elements of the formula for the requisite courage we need. I am convinced that people who experience Abrahamic courage will be set free from oppressive "isms," from life-diminishing addictions, and from incarceration in prisons of pride, prejudice, and fear. They will find the strength to reach out and receive the blessings life has in store for them.

First let us turn to Abraham's call to service. The opening sentence in the Bible in the Book of Genesis is: "In the beginning when God created the heavens and the earth . . ." (Genesis 1:1). The Creator God is the Great Initiator. As in the creation, so it was with Abraham, God took the initiative. The plan to form a covenant people who would embody God's righteousness and loving kindness had been started with Noah and his sons (Genesis 6–10). Then Abraham's father Terah, the son of Shem, one of Noah's sons, is led to journey toward Haran. Now I know all of these names seem as dull and uninspiring as the biblical genealogies with their lists of "begats." But there is a crucial point to my name-calling here. It shows that the God who called Abraham is a long-range planner. The seeds of new beginnings are planted in generations long before they blossom and bear fruit. For example, Abraham's father journeys toward Canaan but makes it only as far as Haran and there he dies. Then God calls Abraham to complete the journey all the way to Canaan to a place which would later be made known as the land of promise. Abraham accepts the call and prepares to go forth leaving behind his country, his kindred, and his father's house. So we ask once again, what gave him the courage to do so? The God who called him had taken the initiative to place him in a venturing tradition and had nurtured in him the trust to embrace the call and to believe in the promise.

When God calls we can be confident that the power is there to respond. The hazards and risks of the assignment may stagger our imagination. Doubt, fear, and dread may suggest our inadequacy. Venturing into uncharted territory may raise the level of one's vulnerability to what would normally be unacceptable levels. But dare to believe with Abraham that the power comes with the call and not only power but promises as well. An invitation to be a part of God's plan is filled with grace. Blessings beyond our deserving are assured because God's presence and providential care are attendants on the journey. And if we falter or lose faith along the way, what then? Abraham has an answer to that question. When Abraham and Sarah went down to Egypt, Abraham feared that Pharaoh would kill him so that he could take his beautiful wife Sarah. In that moment of insecurity Abraham asked his wife to pretend to be his sister. When the Pharaoh was told that Sarah was Abraham's sister, he was then free to make her his wife. Notwithstanding the deception, God stepped in to save the day. God afflicted Pharaoh's household with great plagues, revealing that it was all because of Abraham's deception about Sarah. Then Pharaoh, I think, must have chided Abraham saying . . . "here is your wife, take her, and get out of here!" My sense of Abraham's musings may have sounded something like a confession: "My lapse of confidence in God's protection caused me to put Sarah's life in

jeopardy to save my own hide. I should have been disquali-
fied, the promises should have been revoked. The plan
should have been cancelled. God should have punished me,
but Pharaoh's house instead was the one that was plagued. It
wasn't fair but in God's plan there was a requirement that I
go forth from that place. How strange the ways of God. I now
know that God's plans are stronger than my weaknesses. I
desperately want to be faithful and to be true to the covenant
relationship and the call no matter what the cost." After this
miraculous intervention, Abraham recovered a deepened
sense of his call from God to go forth.

A second feature of the relationship that gave Abraham
the courage to go forth was the intimate dialogue between
Abraham and God.

Abraham, the father of our faith, is also referred to
as "servant of God" (Genesis 26:24) and "friend of God"
(2 Chronicles 20:7). The courageous manner of his service
must have been a reflection of the very intimate relationship
of Abraham and God. The quality of the communication
between them had marks of close friendship. We know how
difficult it is to describe exactly how mature couples convey to
each other what is in their hearts. Different people of faith
vary in their accounts of how God speaks to them. Whatever
the process or mechanism of exchange, God talked to Abraham so clearly that what was said by-passed his filters of
doubt. When he was truly listening he got it and knew that this
was God's word. That kind of clarity is a powerful stimulus
toward courage. When God told him to go forth, he went.
When God told him to go outside and look up at the sky to
count the stars, he went. When God told him to offer up his

son Isaac, Abraham set out with his son and his servants for Mount Moriah. The instructions were clear; his response was prompt and resolute whenever he heard the Hebrew words "lek leka," which means "go forth." But this was not one-way communication. Abraham spoke his heart to God as well. Most frequently he offered prayers of thanksgiving when he worshipped at the altars he had built. At other times, he dared to express disappointment about the delay in the fulfillment of the promise. He complained that he and Sarah were getting too old for even a miracle rejuvenation and that his servant Eliezer would probably have to become his heir. When Abraham spoke, God listened and responded with words renewing the promise or with dramatic reassurance that "nothing is too hard for God." And that renewed his courage to obey the call.

Sometimes I think we would be more courageous if we could be as certain that we were hearing the voice of God. Is it because we are not living in the Bible days when such messages were delivered by angels, or in visions and dreams? I cannot really be sure but I suspect that the great difficulty for us may be that, in our advanced stage of secularization, something is blocking the tradition of cultivating a listening ear and a receptive heart. The best we can seem to do is to get "a rumor of angels"[4] to use the title phrase of Peter Berger's book. We all must agree that there is a lot of static these days between earth and heaven. Yet, remember there was a time even in the so-called Bible days when it was acknowledged that "the word of the Lord was rare in those days: visions were not widespread" (1 Samuel 3:1b).

Set aside for a moment questions about being really sure we are discerning the will of God in certain circumstances.

Perhaps the more serious problem has to do with when it is abundantly clear what God would have us do. Do we have the courage then? To change our outlook? To distance ourselves from social patterns that we know are beneath God's standard of love? To champion an unpopular cause because it is right? Or to go forth into uncomfortable places because we feel called by God? It took courage for Sojourner Truth and Harriet Tubman to make the journey below the Mason-Dixon line to help free the slaves or President Lincoln to sign the Emancipation Proclamation or Mrs. Roosevelt to promote racial equality or Jane Addams to press for woman suffrage or M.L. King Jr. and Rabbi Heschel to march together in Alabama for justice or Oscar Romero to celebrate the Mass in the face of certain death in El Salvador or the late Ted Kennedy championing the cause of the poor or Nelson Mandela confronting the evil system of apartheid. Even when God's call is as clear as crystal, courage may be the key to our going forth. People of faith have different ways of having a heart-to-heart encounter with God. But the wonder of wonders is that God seems to find a way to hear us and speak to us with sufficient clarity that we are able to press our way, knowing that we are not alone.

Thirdly, the God who calls us gives the spiritual assurance enabling us to trust His faithfulness and power to see us through and fulfill the promise. All of us who are members of the Abrahamic tradition are living proof that God is able to provide what has been promised. We are a part of the innumerable host of the lineage of Abraham. In the Book of Hebrews, Chapter 11, which enumerates heroes and heroines of our faith, this entry is made for Abraham:

> By faith he received power of procreation, even though he was too old—and Sarah herself was barren—because he considered him faithful who had promised. Therefore, from one person, and this one as good as dead, descendants were born, "as many as the stars of heaven and as the innumerable grains of sand by the seashore" (Hebrews 11:11–12).

Abraham is commended because of his confidence that the one who had promised was faithful. On one occasion when it seemed very unlikely that the promise of an heir could be fulfilled, God called Abraham to go outside and count the stars, assuring him that his descendants would be as numerous as the stars above. And the text says; "And he believed the Lord, the Lord reckoned it to him as righteousness" (Genesis 15:6). But I want to say a special word for Sarah also. We used to overlook the fact that, in the verses we have just quoted from the Book of Hebrews, Sarah was barely sandwiched into the story and even then reference is made to her barrenness rather than her fruitfulness.

That kind of thing happens all the time in a patriarchal society. Women are considered optional extras in the drama of life. Not so in this story. She was a main character who introduced a major theme of God's gift of life to barren women. This is a common theme with three of the most central matriarchs: Sarah (Genesis 11:30), Rebecca (Genesis 25:21), and Rachel (Genesis 29:31). It is in situations of barrenness that God's power to provide heirs of the promise is displayed most dramatically. God engages Sarah in personal conversation asking her why she laughed at the news that she was to bear a son. She denied that she had laughed. But I suspect even God recognized how ludicrous it was for a ninety-year-old woman to be walking around pregnant. Do you imagine that God noticed the way the text in Hebrews marginalizes so important a character in the narrative? I think so. Although like Abraham, she wasn't perfect, she nevertheless was not excluded from God's plan of creating an alternative community to be the people of the covenant. She, too, had experienced God's call to service, had engaged in intimate personal dialogue, and had seen the mighty hand of God intervene in the case of Abraham's deception of the Pharaoh. She had watched the blessings of prosperity come to her family. There is no need to overlook the fact that she had been cruel to Hagar and later to Ishmael, Hagar's son. But at heart she wanted to help God fulfill the promise, by allowing her handmaiden to bear a son to Abraham. It was not too long before Sarah learned that it is better to follow the Lord's initiative. Her faith was also tested as a mother the day Abraham and their only son Isaac went up the mountain to sacrifice. She noticed that the lamb had been left behind. Had Abraham told her what he thought God was telling him to do—to prove his faith in God by sacrificing his son, Isaac? Was it really God's voice or another spirit urging Abraham to sacrifice his son? Had God calmed Sarah's nerves assuring her that "I will provide"? She had to be asking in her heart, will God really be able to keep the promise and make a way to save the life of Isaac, our son? It must have felt like an eternity while she waited for the answer. And the answer did come. Can you even imagine the exhilaration and the uncontrollable joy when she caught sight of Abraham and Isaac coming down the mountain together? Now she knew beyond a shadow of a doubt that nothing is too hard for God, that she could trust God to provide what is promised.

And by the way, what about Abraham? As he and his son were going up the mountain, Isaac had said to his father, "The fire and the wood are here, but where is the lamb for a burnt offering"? Was it Abraham speaking or was it God's voice within him that said, "God (sic) will provide the lamb for a burnt offering, my son. So the two of them walked on together"(Genesis 22:8). Was there ever such anguish of conscience, soul, or spirit of a father walking with a son on the way to worship God? Then came one of the most heart-wrenching verses in the Bible: "When they came to the place that God had shown him, Abraham built an altar there and laid the wood in order. He bound his son Isaac, and laid him on the altar on top of the wood" (Genesis 22:9). As Abraham was lifting his knife to slay his son, God called his name twice; "Abraham, Abraham." And he said, "Here I am." And the voice of the Lord said, "Do not lay your hand on the boy or do anything to him for now I know that you fear God, since you have not withheld your son, your only son from me"(Genesis 22:12).

When Abraham looked around he saw a ram caught by its horns in the thicket. He sacrificed the ram and he and his son joined the servants and descended from the mountain. But let us go back for a moment to God's deliverance of Isaac. When Abraham was untying his son, how long did he embrace him? Oh, how intense the sobbing, as tears of the son mingled with those of his father. Could the son find words or breath to voice his confusion, bewilderment, and dismay along with his gratitude for the voice of the angel of the Lord which had snatched him from the jaws of death? And what did Abraham say to God? Was it just "Thank You, Thank You!"? Oh no, he named that place "The Lord will provide." He knew he was a servant of a God who was able to provide what was promised. He would live the rest of his life going forth at the Lord's command with trust, courage, and hope.

In conclusion, let us apply this story to our lives:

The story of Abraham belongs to all of us. If we review our own traditions, we should be able to see that his DNA of courage, trust, and blessedness can be found in our spiritual genome. As a Christian, I have found Jesus to personify that courage, communion, and trust in God which we have observed in Father Abraham. Jesus received the call to go forth from the realm of glory to sojourn with us in our pilgrimage of faith. In our midst, he lived the steadfast love of God that was determined to make us whole and to form us into a blessed, beloved community. Jesus found his place in God's plan and in the prophetic branch of his faith. He declared the same in his hometown synagogue when he read from Isaiah 61:

> The Spirit of the Lord is upon me,
> because he has anointed me
> to bring good news to the poor.
> He has sent me to proclaim release to
> the captives and recovery of sight to the blind,
> to let the oppressed go free,
> to proclaim the year of the Lord's favor (Luke 4:18–19).

In saying, "Today this scripture has been fulfilled in your hearing"(Luke 4:21), Jesus was declaring readiness to "go forth." He knew the perils on the path he had chosen but he was confident that the God who had sent him and who was in constant communion with him would be able to fulfill the promise of redemption through his strength, his brokenness, and even his death. In the Garden of Gethsemane, he wrestled like Abraham to be sure that his path was in line with God's plan for humankind and all creation. He died on a cross and was placed in a stone cold tomb. But he was confident that even in the tomb he would hear the call, "lek leka"—"go forth." He heard the call and rose to the glorious occasion of resurrection, as promised.

Do you hear the call? What is the plan of God regarding the issues we face in this time of barrenness? If we are able to discern clearly the path to which God is calling us, would we find the courage to go forth in bold witness? There will be many voices addressing the issues of sexual behavior, gender equality, economic fairness, racial justice, the prospect of war as a path to peace, and the urgency to answer the call to environmental responsibility. When we find our place in God's plan, the wisest course of action is to take courage and to go forth on the path of promise. Abraham and the God-trusting people of his larger family—Jews, Christians, and Muslims— have pre-certified for us that the God who calls us to go forth is faithful and will be with us on the journey.

BENEDICTION
Go forth in the name of the Lord
To spread glad tidings abroad

The love that you share and the witness you bear
Will bring honor and glory to God.

Go forth with a joyful amen
Until we gather again
Remember the word your spirit has heard
God's love is the hope of the world.
Amen.

Acknowledgments

J ust as preaching is more of a communal happening than some people are aware, writing about one's faith perspective is always a report on a team process. One's point of view, strongly held convictions, and even unresolved theological positions take shape in formal and informal settings of study, dialogue, service, worship, or conversations with family and friends. Talk shows, television programs, readings, and other sources of learning and information provide significant input into our faith formation. The culture itself with its broadly held values and moral guidelines is a principal shaper of conscience, attitude and behavior. Thus a vast array of teachers, mentors and unknown contributors deserve a word of appreciation for the thoughts shared in this book.

General thanks are due to my parents and family, friends, teachers, students, classmates, fellow workers, religious leaders and congregations where I have worshipped or served as pastor, teacher, or preacher.

Because I have had strong connections to several broad spiritual movements, I want to express gratitude to the following for the seeds they have sown into my heart and mind: the black pentecostal church of my childhood, particularly the United Holy Church of America and The Church of God in

Christ; the charismatic movement with its emphasis on the gifts of the Spirit; mainline denominations which welcomed me into their pulpits and their annual conferences, particularly the American Baptist Churches which warmly received me into their family and the United Church of Christ with which we had dual alignment at The Riverside Church; and finally the ecumenical interfaith progressive movement which is my present place of spiritual sojourn and exploration. I have been gifted and nurtured by each of the streams of faith with which I have been identified.

More particularly, I am indebted to several institutions and on-going groups where there was the opportunity to share general ideas, papers, projects, and critical reflections on cutting-edge issues demanding thoughtful response and collective action:

Union Theological Seminary, which gave me the finest education possible to prepare me for broad ecumenical ministry, inclining me toward pastoral service and prophetic witness.

Colgate-Rochester Divinity School for its Martin Luther King Jr. Program in Black Church Studies, linking some of the strongest black pastors with an extraordinarily dedicated and resourced faculty directed by Dr. Henry H. Mitchell.

Auburn Theological Seminary, where the opportunity to serve on the core teaching staff provided the richest exchange of ideas and avant-garde thinkers in the field of theology and congregational studies under President Barbara Wheeler's exciting and intellectually stimulating leadership—now followed by Katharine Henderson as President and her commitment to interfaith relations, vibrant congregations, and the empowerment of women—and Auburn Media under the direction of Macky Alston for training and support services for media outreach.

The Partnership of Faith in the City of New York, co-chaired by Arthur Caliandro and myself and now chaired by Peter Rubinstein, where Protestants, Catholics, Muslims, and Jews fellowshipped and shared insights about more effective ways to uplift the quality of life in our city and gave us the opportunity to understand our enriching differences and the common threads of faith that made us friends and colleagues.

The Dialogue Group organized by Edie Beaujon, which convened once or twice a year to think critically about what is happening in our country and how we can best serve as effective change agents.

The Hampton Minister's Conference, where the largest gathering of African American ministers takes place to be inspired and informed by great preaching, teaching, and music.

The Samuel Dewitt Proctor Conference, which gathers annually one of the most prophetically inclined network of pastors and seminarians to prepare for reflection and action for peace, justice, and compassion.

Chautauqua Institution in upstate New York and its Department of Religion under the direction of Joan Brown Campbell for providing an excellent environment for public issues and dialogue on matters of faith.

New York Theological Seminary and President Dale Irvin for opening the doors of Sing Sing Prison for me to participate in the certificate program preparing inmates for ministry.

The Interfaith Metropolitan Education, Inc., in Washington, DC, better known as Intermet Seminary, where I had the opportunity to begin interfaith educational leadership as Director of Education under the guidance of presdent John Fletcher.

The College of Preachers later called Cathedral College at the Washington National Cathedral in Washington, DC, where I presented homiletic workshops and leadership retreats in a peaceful setting so superb for reflection and writing.

Friends and followers of The Healing of the Nations Foundation who supported this project as a part of our mission to bring healing across the various divides in our nation.

The Riverside Church in the City of New York, which for eighteen years was for me a wonderful and challenging congregation to work with through the problems of liberalism, racial inclusion, multicultural understanding, and the crisis of progressive spirituality in a time of social, economic and political upheavals, and paradigm shifts in the nature of contemporary church life.

In regards to the writing of this volume, I want to express my gratitude to Susan Fuhrman, President of Columbia University's Teachers College and attorney Bill Wachtel of the law firm of Wachtel and Masyr, both in New York City, for providing pro-bono space for research and writing.

In appreciation for their research, reflection, editing or typing, I thank Karen Leahy, Evelyn Davis, Elizabeth Hurston, Shannon Daley-Harris, Lese Dutton, Myrtle Shaw, Betty Davis and Michele Ivey and especially Barbara George, Chief of Staff at The Healing of the Nations Foundation who actually became project manager for the book and filled many roles with her theological understanding and literary expertise.

I have been immeasurably enriched by the writings of and conversations with friends with whom I am in dialogue even when we are not together: Charles Adams, Steve Bauman, Nathan Baxter, Harry Belafonte, Richard Berman, Delrio Berry, Marcus Borg, Eric Braverman, Brad Braxton, +Balfour Brickner,° +Ray Brown, +Delwin Brown, John Buchanan, Kenyon Burke, Johnny Bush, Calvin Butts, Joan Brown Campbell, Bob Carpenter, Joan Chittister, +Forrest Church, Jim Clark, Jim Cone, Herbert Daughtry, Fred Dennard, Gary Dorrien, Joyce Dudley, Michael Eric Dyson, Floyd Flake, David and Ronald Forbes, Welton Gaddy, Peter Gomes, +Robert Gumbs, Lee Hancock, +Robert T. Handy, Katherine Henderson, Obery Hendricks, Carter Heyward, Joe Hough, Steven Jacobs, Sujay Johnson-Cook, Arthur Jones, +Miles Jones, Serene Jones, Will Kennedy, John Kinney, Carolyn Knight, Doug Krantz, My literary agent Robert Levine, Elroy Lewis, Barbara Lundblad, Elliott Mason, Ellen McGraff, Ken Medema, Henry Mitchell, +Paul Nichols, +Reinhold Niebuhr, Parker Palmer, Chang Park, Robert Pollack, Ray Rafferty, Larry Rasmussen, Feisal Rauf, W. Franklin Richards, Gerard Richardson, +Shelby Rooks, Petero Sabune, David Saperstein, Robert Seymour, Gwen Shepherd, Paul Sherry, Don and Peggy Shriver, Gary Simpson, Jeffrey Slade, Paul Smith, James Stallings, Brenda and Tom Stiers, Irving Stubbs, Gardner C. Taylor, Felicia Thomas, Anna Towns, Edolphus Towns, Janet Walton, +Jim Washington, Bill Webber, Cornel West, Walter Wink, Jeremiah Wright, Marian Wright-Edelman, Alphonso Wyatt, and Johnny Ray Youngblood.

° The symbol "+" before a name denotes those who are deceased.

A special word of thanks to Bill Moyers for consenting to write the foreword for this project and to his wife Judith for their friendship, encouragement, and support of my ministry.

What a rare gift it is to have someone to discern the contours of one's fundamental project. Carlyle Marney[1] once asked me, "Jim, who told you who you are?" In Moyers' foreword you have been given a glimpse of who I am striving to become.

I cannot say enough about Rita Nakashima Brock who first proposed that I should write this book and reviewed scores of my sermons to discern common threads and then patiently reflected with me until clarity began to emerge. With her delicate dance between holding me to deadlines and avoiding paralyzing pressures, she skillfully lured me into the completion of this book. Her editorial genius was a delight to behold. I feel truly blessed to have had the experience of working with her.

My extreme appreciation to The New Press and their commitment to publish manuscripts in the public interest and to Maury Botton who has assembled a great team ably working to make literary resources available that provide ideas and viewpoints under-represented in the mass media.

To my beloved wife Bettye who labored intensely to help bring this book to birth, and to my talented son James for his candid and wise observations about ways to be effective in ministry, I wish to give thanks for their enduring love and support for me and their role in every aspect of our shared ministry.

Notes

INTRODUCTION

1. Martin Luther King Jr., *Stride Toward Freedom: The Montgomery Story* (New York: Harpers Brothers, 1958).

2. The Healing of the Nations Foundation, founded by the author, promotes the call to each person to be a leaf of healing by making a conscientious commitment to self-care and to the care of others. As instruments of healing, individuals and communities become a compassionate voice and a committed force that promotes health, peace, justice, interfaith parnerships, and environmental responsibility. For more information, visit the Web site: www.healingofthenations.com.

CHAPTER 1: A LIFELONG COURSE IN SEXUALITY

1. Levirate marriage (*yibbum*). A Jewish custom which obliges a childless widow to marry her dead husband's brother. The obligation of levirate marriage is laid down in Deuteronomy 25:5–6 (John Bowker, *The Concise Oxford Dictionary of World Religions* [New York: Oxford University Press, 1997]).

2. Excerpted from a poem protesting America's war with Mexico by James R. Lowell, published in the *Boston Courier*, December 11, 1845.

3. "Charismatic Conference" is a part of an ecumenical movement dedicated to the experience and the gifts of the spirit beyond traditional Pentecostal churches.

CHAPTER 2: GENDER EQUALITY

1. Rosemary Radford Ruether, *Sexism and God-Talk: Toward a Feminist Theology* (Boston: Beacon Press, 1993).
2. Ibid., 24.
3. Peter J. Gomes, *The Good Book: Reading the Bible with Mind and Heart* (New York: HarperCollins Publishers, Inc., 1996).
4. Ibid., 143.

CHAPTER 3: WHICH GOSPEL DO YOU BELIEVE ABOUT RACE?

1. Will Counts, Will Campbell, Ernest Dumas, and Robert S. McCord, *A Life Is More Than a Moment* (Bloomington, IN: Indiana University Press, 1999).
2. Maya Angelou, *The Complete Collected Poems of Maya Angelou* (New York: Random House, 1994), 224.
3. William Sloane Coffin, *A Passion for the Possible* (Louisville, KY: Westminter John Knox Press, 1993).
4. Produced and available from Ebb Pod Productions, P.O. Box 380302, Cambridge, MA 02238, e-mail: *info@tracesofthetrade.org*.

CHAPTER 4: ECONOMIC JUSTICE

1. Excerpted remarks from "Education for the Human Spirit" by Norman Lear to the National Education Association's National Convention, Kansas City, Missouri, July 7, 1990.

CHAPTER 5: IN WAR

1. Former pastor of the Concord Baptist Church of Brooklyn, New York.

2. Henry Emerson Fosdick, *The Living of These Days* (New York: Harper & Brothers, 1956), 304.

3. Glen H. Stassen, *Just Peacemaking: Transforming Initiatives for Justice and Peace* (Louisville, KY: Westminster John Knox, 1992), p 112.

4. Edwina Hunter, ordained in the American Baptist Church, is a distinguished preacher in America. She recently retired from her position as the Joe R. Engle Professor of Preaching at Union Theological Seminary in New York City. She is a past president of the Academy of Homiletics, the editor of a volume of women's sermons, and has had numerous sermons published in other volumes.

CHAPTER 6: CRITIQUE, CONFESSION, AND ECOLOGICAL CONSCIOUSNESS

1. Matthew Fox, Joseph Sittler, Annie Dillard, and others. Interestingly, as early as 1972, John Cobb asked a question that has only gained urgency with the passage of time in his book *Is It Too Late? A Theology of Ecology.*

2. Quoted in Fritjof Capra, *The Web Of Life: A New Scientific Understanding of Living Systems* (New York: Anchor/Doubleday Books, 1996), xi.

3. Unpublished song, "Song of the Heavens," by the author.

4. Author's note: shalom is used here in its fullest context—to be at peace with one's God, one's world, one's community and oneself makes possible the radical reform needed today.

EPILOGUE

1. I usually begin my sermons with a clear statement of the sermonic theme to be developed and also what I hope the hearers will derive from the sermon. In this sermon, the text and proposition are as follows:

Text: Genesis 12:1-4 and Luke 4:16-21 (All scripture references are from the New Revised Standard Version of the Bible.)

Proposition: I propose to show that the courage to "go forth" as a part of God's plan comes from a relationship with God which enables us to experience God's call to service, engage in intimate dialogue with God, and to trust God's faithfulness and power to provide what has been promised—to the end that the hearers will be:

    1) alert to the God who calls and provides the strength to respond;

    2) aware that believing and trusting God's promise is the heart of righteousness;

    3) assured that God works through our strength and weaknesses to fulfill both promise and plan.

2. Gerhard Von Rad, *Genesis: A Commentary/Old Testament Library* (Philadelphia: Westminster Press, 1961).

3. Walter Brueggemann, *Genesis: Interpretation: A Bible Commentary for Teaching and Preaching* (Atlanta: John Knox Press, 1982).

4. Peter Berger, *A Rumor of Angels: Modern Society and the Rediscovery of the Supernatural* (New York: Knopf Doubleday Publishing Group, 1970).

ACKNOWLEDGMENTS

1. Carlyle Marney, now deceased, served as Pastor of Myers Park Baptist Church in Charlotte, North Carolina.